FIFTH EDITION

Student Workbook to Accompany

THE
LITIGATION
PARALEGAL

A Systems Approach

JAMES W.H. McCORD
SANDRA L. McCORD

D1303904

⊹ **DELMAR**
CENGAGE Learning™

Australia • Brazil • Japan • Korea • Mexico • Singapore • Spain • United Kingdom • United States

DELMAR
CENGAGE Learning

**Student Workbook to Accompany
The Litigation Paralegal: A Systems
Approach, Fifth Edition**
James W.H. McCord and Sandra L. McCord

For product information and technology assistance, contact us at
Cengage Learning Customer & Sales Support, 1-800-354-9706

For permission to use material from this text or product,
submit all requests online at **cengage.com/permissions**
Further permissions questions can be e-mailed to
permissionrequest@cengage.com

Library of Congress Control Number: 2006101408

ISBN-13: 978-1-4180-1608-1

ISBN-10: 1-4180-1608-X

Delmar
5 Maxwell Drive
Clifton Park, NY 12065-2919
USA

Cengage Learning products are represented in Canada by Nelson Education, Ltd.

For your lifelong learning solutions, visit **delmar.cengage.com**

Visit our corporate website at **cengage.com**

Notice to the Reader

Publisher does not warrant or guarantee any of the products described herein or perform any independent analysis in connection with any of the product information contained herein. Publisher does not assume, and expressly disclaims, any obligation to obtain and include information other than that provided to it by the manufacturer. The reader is expressly warned to consider and adopt all safety precautions that might be indicated by the activities herein and to avoid all potential hazards. By following the instructions contained herein, the reader willingly assumes all risks in connection with such instructions. The Publisher makes no representation or warranties of any kind, including but not limited to, the warranties of fitness for particular purpose or merchantability, nor are any such representations implied with respect to the material set forth herein, and the publisher takes no responsibility with respect to such material. The Publisher shall not be liable for any special, consequential, or exemplary damages resulting, in whole or part, from the readers' use of, or reliance upon, this material.

Printed in the United States of America
6 7 8 9 15 14 13 12

CONTENTS

INTRODUCTION

This workbook is a valuable learning resource closely integrated with the text *The Litigation Paralegal: A Systems Approach, Fifth Edition,* by James W. H. McCord, published by Thomson Delmar Learning. Each chapter includes the following sections:

1. Chapter Objective. Here you will find the goal that should be accomplished by the end of your work on this chapter.

2. Chapter Outline. This will help you identify the main divisions of the chapter for a quick overview as you approach the chapter and for review as you complete it. Use the outline to help organize your class notes.

3. Define. This list of key terms from the chapter gives you space to write their definitions in your own words to test and increase your understanding. These terms are identified in bold print in the chapter, where they are defined in context. You can also find them in the text glossary. You may choose to add other terms from the text or from class notes.

4. Workbook Assignments and Exercises. Here you will find the System Folder Assignments, Application Assignments, Internet Exercises, and Additional Exercises to strengthen your understanding and experience. Space and formats are provided for these assignments. Whether assigned by your instructor or completed for your own enrichment, the assignments and exercises are designed to enhance your learning experience substantially and to help you compile your system folder more efficiently.

5. Chapter Review Tests and Answers. This is a quick overview of the chapter in the form of fill in the blank, true/false, multiple choice, and short answer questions. Use the test and answers to gauge your progress and to help identify areas needing additional study. The chapter tests can be combined to aid your preparation for unit, mid-term, and final exams.

As you apply yourself to the tasks included in this workbook, remember that you are not just filling out forms and answering questions. You are building a body of knowledge— a litigation system that will help you become a skilled and responsible professional in the field of law.

James W. H. McCord
Sandra L. McCord

Chapter 1. WELCOME TO THE LAW OFFICE: FOUNDATIONS FOR LITIGATION

Chapter Objective

The purpose of this chapter is to give you a feeling that you are starting work in a law office. The first section provides case "stories" that demonstrate the kinds of events that may lead to litigation. The stories give the necessary factual settings for many of the assignments and examples in the text, and bring them to life.

The Paralegal Handbook section is "the firm's" introduction to the office, its personnel, the role of the paralegal, important procedures, professional ethics, and professional development. It also introduces the systems approach. The section following the handbook provides an introduction to (or review of) court structure, jurisdiction, and venue.

Outline

I.   Introduction
    A.   Case II, *Forrester v. Richard Hart and Mercury Parcel Service, Inc.*
    B.   Case II, *Ameche v. Congden*
    C.   Case III, *Coleman v. Make Tracks, Inc.*
    D.   Case IV, *Briar Patch Dolls, Inc. v. Teeny Tiny Manufacturing Co.*
    E.   Case V, *Rakowski v. Montez Construction Co.*

II. Office Manual

III. The Paralegal Handbook: Office Orientation and Ethics
    A.   Structure and Personnel
        1.   Titles/Diversity
        2.   The Changing Law Office
        3.   The Work of the Firm
        4.   The Role of the Paralegal
    B.   Important Law Office Procedures
        1.   Introduction
        2.   Timekeeping and Billing
        3.   Disbursement (Expense) Entry
        4.   Deadline (Docket) Control
        5.   Technology Management
        6.   E-mail
        7.   Technology Security
    C.   Techniques for Thriving in the Law Office
    D.   The Training Procedure
        1.   Procedure, Task Information, Assignments
        2.   Developing a Litigation System
    E.   Ethical and Other Professional Responsibilities
        1.   Introduction
        2.   What a Paralegal May Not Do
        3.   What a Paralegal May Do
        4.   Confidentiality, Honesty, Conflict of Interest, and Other Ethical Considerations
        5.   Other Professional Considerations
    F.   Your Professional Development

Define

Civil litigation

_____

_____

Multijurisdictional practice

_____

_____

Billable hours

_____

_____

Electronic billing (e-billing)

_____

_____

Unbundling legal services

_____

_____

Litigation system

_____

_____

Professional ethics

_____

_____

Legal advice

_____

_____

Pro bono

_____

_____

Chapter One: Welcome to the Law Office

Jurisdictional amount

_____

Jurisdiction

_____

Geographical

_____

Personal

_____

Subject matter

_____

General

_____

Original

_____

Limited

_____

Exclusive

_____

Supplemental

_____

Removal

_____

Concurrent

_____

Alienage

_____

Federal question

_____

Diversity of citizenship

_____

Domicile

_____

Writ of certiorari

_____

Venue

_____

Workbook Assignments and Exercises

System Folder Assignments

1.   Set up a three-ring binder (or electronic equivalent) with the tab dividers arranged as described in the litigation system section of the text. Copies of the office structure and forms previously discussed should be placed in the system folder as indicated in Appendix A. Begin a table of contents for your system folder and add any information assigned by your instructor.

2.   Look up your state's ethical rules that govern confidentiality, conflict of interest, attorney supervision of lay persons and legal assistants, professional integrity, and others. Record the rule numbers in an ethics section of your system folder. Look up your state's unauthorized practice of law statute; note the wording and the possible penalties. You might want to add this to your folder. As you read further in this text and in other sources, insert in your folder the citations for key ethical rules and guidelines.

3.   Locate the names, addresses, and phone numbers of your local and state paralegal associations. If you need help obtaining this information, try the director of a local paralegal program or any experienced paralegal. The headquarters of the state bar association might also have such information. For future reference, you may choose to place your expanded lists of sources for professional development in your system folder.

State Paralegal Association	Local Paralegal Association
Name:	Name:
Address:	Address:
Phone:	Phone:
E-Mail:	E-Mail:
Web Site:	Web Site:
Contact Person:	Contact Person:
Meeting Dates and Times:	Meeting Dates and Times:

4.   Make a copy of the federal court structure diagram found in the text and add any explanatory notes you feel will be useful to you in the future. Include in your diagram the names of U.S. district courts that sit in your state and the U.S. Court of Appeals that covers the circuit in which your state is situated.

Make a similar explanatory diagram for the court system of your state. Research the material to be placed in the diagram, including any jurisdictional amounts, by looking under courts, judiciary, and jurisdiction in the index of your state statutes or constitution, usually located in the law library, or search your State Court Web site. Some states have an administrative office of the courts at the capitol, which may provide preprinted state court diagrams.

Place both diagrams and the State Court Web site address in the court section of your litigation system folder.

5.   Consult the state's legal directory in the library or online sites to obtain all court addresses, names of clerks of court, important telephone numbers, and so on. Research state statutes for the subject matter jurisdiction of your state's highest, intermediate, and trial courts. Place this data in the court structure portion of your system folder.

Federal Court System	Address:
Highest Court	Clerk:
Name:	Phone:
Jurisdiction:	
Intermediate Appellate Court	Address:
Name:	Clerk:
Jurisdiction:	Phone:
Trial Courts	Address:
Name:	Clerk:
Jurisdiction:	Phone:
State Court System	
Highest Court	Address:
Name:	Clerk:
Jurisdiction:	Phone:
Intermediate Appellate Court	Address:
Name:	Clerk:
Jurisdiction:	Phone:
Trial Courts	Address:
Name:	Clerk:
Jurisdiction:	Phone:

Application Assignments

1.   To develop a timekeeping habit during this training period, keep track of your time spent on assignments on the following Time Log, similar to that in Exhibit 1:2. Use a separate notebook or loose-leaf paper that can be placed at the back of your system folder or keep track of your time in an electronic timekeeping program, if one is available.

BG	Budgeting	DM	Document	M	Memorandum	SE	Settlement
C	Conference		Management	MO	Motion	T	Telephone
CT	Court	DS	Discovery	P	Preparation	TR	Travel
D	Document	I	Investigation	PL	Planning	O	Other
	Drafting	L	Letter	R	Research		

TIME LOG   Name_____

Case no.	Service	Comment	Date	Hours by 10ths

2.   Set up a simple deadline calendar for this training period. Use any type of standard calendar. Enter all important deadlines such as assignment due dates and exam dates. Use a system of advance reminder dates prior to the actual deadline and post-deadline reminders for necessary corrective action.

_____
_____
_____
_____

3.   An attorney relied on a non-attorney calendar clerk to let him know when a notice of appeal was due. The deadline was missed, and the attorney filed for an extension of time because of excusable neglect, allowable if there is good cause for the mistake. Should the extension be granted?

_____
_____
_____
_____

4.   Using the ethical standards and rules cited in the text, answer the following questions on ethics.
     a.   You have just researched an issue and have found that inattentive driving is a breach of the duty of care that a driver owes to others. In a phone conversation the client asks you, "If the driver of the vehicle that struck me was inattentive, is he in the wrong?" How should you answer?

_____
_____
_____
_____

     b.   Ms. Pearlman asks you to draft a release of medical information form for a client. This form is drafted and signed by the client and given to the hospital. Under what conditions can you do this and avoid the unauthorized practice of law?

_____
_____
_____
_____

     c.   You are working on a client's case for Ms. Pearlman. She is gone, so you want to consult with Mr. White, another attorney in our firm. To do so, however, you must reveal to Mr. White some confidential information about the client. Would this be a breach of confidentiality?

_____
_____
_____
_____

     d.   You are a paralegal working for an attorney who has represented Safe Bet Insurance Company. A potential client wants to sue Safe Bet. Is there a potential conflict of interest, and if so, may your attorney represent the new client?

_____
_____
_____
_____

e.   In interviewing a client, you and your attorney are convinced that some informa-tion provided by the client is false. What consequences can result from the presentation of such information to the court? What model rule of professional conduct applies?

_____

_____

_____

_____

f.   Your supervising attorney asks you to release to the press a letter from a third party. The attorney says, "I'll finally get even by truly embarrassing the s.o.b." What should you do?

_____

_____

_____

_____

5.   Determine in which courts subject matter jurisdiction, personal jurisdiction, and venue exist in the following problems.
    a.   A, a resident of Florida, sues B, a resident of Washington, who is also the secretary of the interior, in a First Amendment freedom of speech issue arising in southeast Georgia.

_____

_____

_____

_____

b.   M, a resident of Wisconsin, and O, a resident of Minnesota, sue Corporations X and Y for industrial injuries amounting to $40,000 for each plaintiff resulting from an acci-dent that occurred in Illinois. X is incorporated in Delaware and Ohio, and Y is incorpo-rated in North Carolina with its principal place of business in Ohio.

_____

_____

_____

_____

c.   J and K reside in Oregon and sue R, who resides in Kentucky, and S, who resides in Washington, for a tort (libel) amounting to injuries exceeding $75,000 each, which occurred in Washington.

_____

_____

_____

_____

d.   What happens in problem (c) if S is a Canadian citizen living in Louisiana?

_____

_____

_____

_____

e.   E sues Great Britain for damages exceeding $500,000 for the illegal impounding of E's commercial plane.

_____

_____

_____

_____

Internet Exercises

1. Go to http://www.abanet.org. In the search window, type *model guidelines for the utilization of paralegal services*. Find paragraph 3 of the comment to Guideline 1. What must a lawyer do to conform to Guideline 1?

2. Ask your instructor for the name of your state and local paralegal association. Using a general search engine, see if that association has a Web site. If so, note the Web address in your system folder.

3. Go to both the NALA and NFPA Web sites and note the variety of career information available.

4. Using your own search strategy, locate the Web site for your state courts. Note what general categories of information are available and enter this information in your system folder.

Additional Learning Exercises and Discussion Points

1. Without trying to use legal terminology or technical theories, answer the following questions for each of the five hypothetical cases presented in this chapter.
    a. Who is suing and what basis might they have?
    b. Against whom is the suit brought and what defenses might they have?
    c. Who do you think will win and why?

Case I

_____
_____
_____

Case II

_____
_____
_____

Case III

_____
_____
_____

Case IV

_____
_____
_____

Case V

_____
_____
_____

2. Apply the directions for preparing a time slip to enter these activities in the form provided. Assume your hourly rate is $40 an hour and the date is today. Round to nearest tenth of an hour.

> 6 minute phone call to client A. Forrester, Case I.
> 16 minutes to draft letter on behalf of client Heinz, Case IV.
> 1 hour and 18 minutes to research cause of action for client Ameche, Case II.
> 1 hour and 20 minutes to attend continuing education luncheon to improve general knowledge, but which may be useful on Cases III and IV. Cost $5. (Should this be charged to the client?)

Permanent Time Log								
Service Codes								

BG Budgeting   DM Document   M   Memorandum   SE Settlement
C   Conference   Management   MO Motion   T   Telephone
CT Court   DS Discovery   P   Preparation   TR Travel
D   Document   I   Investigation   PL Planning   O   Other
       Drafting   L   Letter   R   Research

No Charge Items

NC No Charge   CE Continuing Education   PS Public Service
B   Bar Function   CR Client Relations

Date	File No.	Client	Att/ Plgl	Serv Code	Hrs	10th	Rate/ Hr	Amt.

Comments:

Out-of-Pocket Expense

3. Fill out disbursement records in the following form based on this information.
    100 photocopies at 10¢ per copy, business records for Heinz, Case IV.
    Trip to investigate accident scene for client McVay, Case X
        $60, motel; $5, lunch; $11, dinner; 100 miles at .25 per mile.
    Computer research time 10 minutes at $5 per minute for Montez Construction, Case V.

Permanent Disbursement Record					
Expense Codes:					

C   Photocopies   L   Lodging   P Postage   T   Telephone
CT   Online Computer   M   Meals $ Cash   TR Travel
ON   Overnight Express   TG Telegrams   O   Other
F   Filing and Other fees

Date	File No.	Client	Atty/Plgl	Exp. Code	Amt.

Comments:

4.   Assume that you have just opened the morning mail and received a copy of a complaint alleging a cause of action against Mr. Holton who is represented by your firm. His file number is 92-1000. You know that you have 20 days starting tomorrow to file an answer and that it is your job to draft an answer for your supervising attorney's review. You have received the complaint on September 5. Making up the names you need, prepare the following deadline control slip so the document will be ready to mail on the 20th day. Ignore the fact that some days may be weekend days for purposes of this assignment only. Assume it will take a half day to research and draft the answer, 1 hour for the attorney to review it, a half hour for you to make revisions, and a half hour for the secretary to type it and have it ready for mailing. Complete all sections of the slip.

Deadline Slip								
Client:			File Number:					
Atty:	Start:	Due:	Plgl:	Start:	Due:	Staff:	Start:	Due:
Task:			Task:			Task:		
Remarks:			Remarks:			Remarks:		
Reminder: 1 2 Final Done:			Reminder: 1 2 Final Done:			Reminder: 1 2 Final Done:		

5.   Of all the techniques mentioned for thriving in the law office, which two are most important? Explain.

_____
_____
_____

6.   Describe a paralegal litigation system folder and its advantages.

_____
_____
_____

7.   Read thoroughly the Model Rules of Professional Conduct or your state rules of conduct to gain a fuller understanding of your ethical responsibilities. Why is confidentiality so important?

_____
_____
_____

8.   Glitter is a corporation that rents expensive jewelry to businesses and individuals. It is incorporated in Delaware and has its principal place of business in Northern Indiana. It is licensed to do business in every state except Alaska and Hawaii. Flick, Inc., is a movie company incorporated in Idaho with its principal place of business in Utah. It does no business to speak of in any other state.

During Flick's filming in Nevada, an expensive necklace rented from Glitter falls into a piece of machinery on the set and is destroyed. Glitter wants to sue Flick for negligently destroying the jewelry (worth $700,000). Flick decides to sue Glitter, blaming the loss of a week's filming on the loss of the necklace, which they claim was caused by a faulty clasp made by Glitter. After using the charting method described in this section, answer the following questions:

GLITTER V. FLICK FOR NECKLACE

Court	Subj. Matter Juris.	Venue	Pers.	Juris.
Delaware State				
Indiana State				
Idaho State				
Utah State				
Nevada State				
Delaware Federal				
Indiana Federal				
Idaho Federal				
Utah Federal				
Nevada Federal				

ISSUE: Is filming a movie in a state a sufficient contact to allow personal service? (May depend on state statutes and overall degree of contacts.)

FLICK V. GLITTER FOR LOSS OF WEEK OF FILMING

Court	Subj. Matter Juris.	Venue	Pers.	Juris.
Delaware State				
Indiana State				
Idaho State				
Utah State				
Nevada State				
Delaware Federal				
Indiana Federal				
Idaho Federal				
Utah Federal				
Nevada Federal				

a. If Glitter sues Flick, is there subject matter jurisdiction in federal district court?

_____

_____

_____

b. What, if any, kind of subject matter jurisdiction exists in federal district court?

_____

_____

_____

c. What issue concerning personal jurisdiction exists when considering suit by Glitter against Flick in Nevada state and federal court?

_____

_____

_____

d. Aside from Nevada, in what state and federal courts can Glitter sue Flick?

_____

_____

_____

e.   If Flick sues Glitter, does venue exist in the state courts of Idaho and Utah? Why or why not?

_____
_____
_____

f.   Assume for purposes of this question that Glitter is licensed to do business in Utah and, thus, is subject to personal jurisdictional in Utah.
   1.   What impact would this have on jurisdictional considerations?

_____
_____
_____

   2.   With the same facts, assume diversity jurisdiction still exists. Could Utah's federal court have venue, considering that the action did not arise in Utah?

_____
_____
_____

g.   What facts are missing in the Flick v. Glitter scenario that affect jurisdiction?

_____
_____
_____

h.   In what state and federal courts can Flick sue Glitter?

_____
_____
_____

9.   Work through the text questions for study and review to test your understanding of the chapter.

_____
_____
_____

Chapter Review Test and Answers

Review Test

Fill in the Blank

1. Attorney-owners of a law firm are called _____; salaried attorneys are _____ or, if they have no expectation of becoming partner, _____. Those who provide legal services under the supervision of an attorney are _____.

2. Good _____ record keeping reduces disputes over fees.

3. Charging a set fee for a particular task is called _____.

4. Law offices are most often sued for malpractice because of _____.

5. Ethical standards are set by _____ and are frequently based on _____.

6. Trial courts decide questions of _____ while appellate courts decide questions of _____.

7. The terms for judges in constitutional courts are _____.

8. The jurisdictional amount for federal diversity cases is _____.

True or False

T F 1.   Paralegals are responsible for clerical and word processing services for the law firm.

T F 2.   Disbursements are expenses incurred on behalf of the client.

T F 3.   Help your client feel comfortable by using first names immediately.

T F 4.   Pro-bono cases are cases involving malpractice.

T F 5.   The U.S. Court of Appeals for the Federal Circuit hears appeals from the U.S. Commissioner of Patents.

T F 6.   U.S. Court of Appeals has original jurisdiction over controversies between two or more states.

T F 7.   An adverse party for whom a newly hired paralegal once worked should be informed of the hiring and of the nature of the conflict of interest screen.

Multiple Choice

1. Industrial espionage might lead to this type of litigation:
   a. contract case
   b. civil rights case
   c. corporation case
   d. products liability case

2. Timekeeping is important for
   a. analyzing productivity
   b. setting speed records
   c. determining billable hours
   d. a. and c.
   e. none of the above

3. A tickler system
   a. helps with legal research
   b. is a calendaring process
   c. keeps law office personnel in a jovial mood
   d. indicates proper venue

4. Professional telephone use includes all the following except:
   a. a chatty conversation
   b. repetition of facts
   c. brevity
   d. identification as a paralegal

5. Paralegals may
   a. give legal advice to a friend
   b. accept cases for the firm
   c. represent clients at federal administrative hearings
   d. split fees with an attorney

6. Florida court decisions and legislation introduced in some states have pointed toward possible changes in rules regarding
   a. unauthorized practice of law
   b. conflict of interest
   c. confidentiality
   d. licensing of paralegals
   e. a and d
   f. all of the above

7. Ethical responsibility in a law firm rests with
   a. attorneys
   b. the senior partner
   c. paralegals
   d. legal secretaries
   e. all of the above

8. A court has personal jurisdiction
   a. when a summons and complaint are served within its geographical district
   b. when a summons and complaint are served out-of-state under a long-arm statute
   c. over everyone in its district
   d. a. and b.
   e. b. and c.

9. Jurisdictional amount
   a. can determine in which court a case can be tried
   b. is the attorney's fee
   c. is the same in all courts
   d. can be waived for indigents

10. Legislative courts include all the following except:
    a. United States Claims Court
    b. United States District Court
    c. United States Tax Court
    d. United States Court of Veterans Appeals

11. Except in class action cases, the jurisdictional amount in federal diversity cases
    a. is the combined claim for multiple plaintiffs
    b. is the value of all claims made by one plaintiff against one defendant
    c. can never include attorney's fees
    d. is the value of each plaintiff's interest in the property in question rather than the actual value of the property

12. Venue is all the following except:
    a. the county where the incident occurred
    b. the county where all the defendants reside
    c. each county where multiple plaintiffs reside
    d. neighborhood

13. The law that substantially extends diversity jurisdiction in class action cases
    a. is the Class Action Fairness Act
    b. is the State Class Action Limitation Act
    c. sets the jurisdictional amount for all plaintiffs combined at $10 million
    d. requires all plaintiffs and defendants to be diverse

Short Answer

1. What is the role of the paralegal in the law firm?

_____
_____
_____

2. What are the consequences of malpractice suits?

_____
_____
_____

3. How is the development of a litigation system important to you?

_____
_____
_____

4. Define conflict of interest as it applies to paralegals.

_____
_____
_____

5. How can a paralegal continue professional development?

_____
_____
_____

6. U.S. District Court has original jurisdiction in what types of cases?

_____
_____
_____

7. What is the domicile of a corporation? An insurance company? A national bank?

_____

_____

_____

8. What is the subject matter jurisdiction of your state courts?

_____

_____

_____

9. Explain the differences between venue and subject matter jurisdiction.

_____

_____

_____

10. How is forum non conveniens used?

_____

_____

_____

Answers to Review Test

Fill in the Blank

1. partners, associates, staff attorneys, paralegals
2. disbursement, billing, or expense
3. task-based billing
4. missed deadlines
5. the state's highest court, the ABA's Model Rules of Professional Conduct
6. law and fact, law
7. for life
8. $75,000

True or False	*Multiple Choice*	
1. F	1. c	8. d
2. T	2. d	9. a
3. F	3. b	10. b
4. F	4. a	11. b
5. T	5. c	12. c
6. F	6. e	13. a
7. T	7. e	

Short Answer

1. Completing tasks assigned by attorneys:
     gathering and organizing information,
     drafting documents,
     researching and investigating,
     assisting at hearings and trials,
     filing matters,
     informing clients on case status,
     generating income for the firm through billable hours,
     benefiting clients through lower rate and efficient work.

2. Higher insurance costs, damaged reputations, disciplinary action by the bar.

3. As a learning process for tasks and organization, as a reference for frequent tasks, and as an asset in obtaining employment.

4. Working for one party when there is already a relationship (former representation, investment, etc.) with the opposing party.

5. a.   Keep informed of what is going on in your field.
   b.   Attend continuing education seminars.
   c.   Participate in paralegal associations.
   d.   Subscribe to paralegal literature.

6. Federal question and diversity of citizenship with amount of $50,000 in controversy.

7. State in which it is incorporated and principal place of business. Insurance, above plus state of insured person. National bank, state designated in its articles of association as its main office.

8. Check your state court diagram

9. Subject matter jurisdiction defines what subject, including amount in dispute, a court is authorized to hear; venue permits a court to hear a case because that is the geographical location in which the defendant lives or in which the cause of action arose. What v. where.

10. To transfer a case to another court having requisite jurisdiction and venue if the original court is inconvenient to the defendant.

 For additional resources, visit our Web site at **http://www.paralegal .delmar.cengage.com.**

Chapter 2. THE INITIAL INTERVIEW

Chapter Objective

The purpose of this chapter is to help you understand the purpose of an initial client interview and to develop a systematic way of preparing for, conducting, and summarizing an interview.
Note: If you have not studied torts and contracts in previous courses or if you need a review of those topics, read Appendices B and C.

Outline

   I. Introduction

  II. The Interview Plan
     A. Interview Plan Checklist
     B. The Interview Plan in Detail
        (A Brief Look at the Substantive Law of Negligence)

 III. The Interview
     A. The Introduction
     B. Questions on Circumstances of the Accident
     C. The Issue of Comparative or Contributory Negligence
     D. The Extent of Injury and Sensitive Inquiry
     E. Dealing with Difficult Clients
     F. Concluding the Interview

 IV. Confirming the Statute of Limitations

  V. Summarizing the Interview

 VI. Keeping the Client Informed

VII. Summary

Define

Substantive law

_____

_____

Procedural law

_____

_____

Duty

_____

_____

Proximate cause

_____

_____

Leading question

_____

_____

Contingent fee

_____

_____

Statute of limitations

_____

_____

Workbook Assignments and Exercises

System Folder Assignments

1.   List the interview tasks and the purposes of the tasks at the beginning of the interview section in your system folder.

2.   Place a copy of the Interview Plan Checklist in your system folder. Add to this section any forms, techniques, examples, or other material that you or your instructor deem useful.

3.   Review the interview forms, noting the type of information requested. Place a copy of these interview forms or similar forms into this section of your system folder.

4.   Review the interview forms in Exhibits 2:1 and 2:2 and compile a list of the names, addresses, phone numbers, medical records, insurance information, and so on, that you would like Ms. Forrester to bring to the interview. Make a copy of the list and place it in the system folder. This list will be useful when you call or write the client and will serve as a checklist for future cases.

5.   Make the letter in Exhibit 2:3 into a form letter for your system folder. Redraft the letter to suit your style and needs, leaving blank those areas of the letter that will contain the variable information (names, addresses, date, and so on) for each new client. Once your form is set up, it can be placed in your system folder requiring the entry of only the variable information for each repeated use. Throughout this training period, follow this form-making procedure for letters and other documents that will be used repeatedly from one case to the next.

Note: Keep track of your time by filling out the time log.

White, Wilson & McDuff
Attorneys at Law
Federal Plaza Building Suite 700
Third and Market Streets
Legalville, Columbia 00000

---

6. List the pertinent ethical considerations for interviewing a client. Place them in your system folder.

7. Prepare a list of the interview techniques in step 8 for your system folder. Add any techniques suggested by your instructor.

8. Your supervising attorney has asked you to develop a draft of a brochure for clients with information the client should receive at the initial interview. Include any additions to the brochure suggested by your instructor. Place the brochure in your system folder.

9. Note in your system folder what forms you should have ready for the client at the initial interview. Include samples of those forms or references to where they can be located quickly, such as the page number in the textbook, the form number in a form file, or in computer files.

10. Develop your own checklist of the items you will need at the interview site. Such a checklist will be a quick reference for preparing your office or a conference room for the interview. Include the necessary forms and directions. Place this material in the system folder.

11. Locate the common statutes of limitations through the index to the state's statutes. Compile a list of the statute numbers and time limits for cases involving personal injury, property damage, wrongful death, contracts (oral and written), and any others requested by your instructor. Place the list into the system folder.

    a. Personal injury   _____ years
         statute number   _____.
    b. Property damage   _____ years
         statute number   _____.
    c. Wrongful death   _____ years
         statute number   _____.
    d. Contracts
         oral   _____ years
         statute number   _____.
         written   _____ years
         statute number   _____.
    e. Others
         _____   _____ years
         statute number   _____.
         _____   _____ years
         statute number   _____.

Application Assignments

1. Test your research skills and learn about your state law by researching the terms *negligence, contributory negligence,* and *comparative negligence* in your state's jury instruction book, statutes, or digest. For additional understanding of these concepts, look in a legal encyclopedia, *Am Jur's Proof of Facts,* or other national reference sources. Note what must be proved.

_____

_____

_____

2.   Adapting the methods you have learned to a variety of circumstances is an important process and an invaluable ability in the law office. Test your understanding of the methodology described in step 2 of planning the interview by creating an interview form for a breach of implied warranty or other type of case. If needed, see the appendix on contracts to review the elements for an implied warranty case. If each student or group of students is to prepare interview forms for different types of lawsuits, it would be good to exchange copies of these forms to expand the interview section of your system folder.

_____

_____

_____

_____

3.   Conduct an interview of Mr. Ameche (Case II). Do this in class in a role-playing setting unless told to do otherwise by your instructor. Divide the interview into various segments (introduction, personal information, events leading up to accident, the accident, injuries, etc.). Different students should take the responsibility of interviewee and interviewer for each segment. The class should critique each segment of the interview according to the following criteria:

1. Friendly and effective introduction
2. Clarity of questions
3. Application of specific interview techniques
4. Willingness to probe
5. Attitude toward client
6. Effective conclusion of interview
7. Overall preparation
8. Sincerity of interviewer

Data Sheet for Mr. Ameche, Case II

If you are assigned the role of Mr. Ameche:

1.   Study the data sheet so that you can respond to questions without having to refer repeatedly to the data sheet. Pay particular attention to the description of the accident.
2.   It would be normal to have to refer to documents to get the names of doctors, hospitals, bills, insurance companies, etc.
3.   Provide your own answers when asked a question for which the data sheet has not provided information. (MU = Make up information)

Has not contacted other attorney
Referred to firm by neighbor
Carl Evan Ameche, Soc. Sec. No. 000-00-0000
2222 2nd St., Thorp, Ohio 10000, Meade County, Phone: MU
Date of Birth: MU Age: 35 Nationality, Race, Religion: MU
Accountant with Miller & Miller 3000 Third St., Thorp $38,000

Married to Zoe Elaine (Jeffers), part-time day care aid and homemaker,
Soc. Sec. No. 000-10-0000 Phone: MU Married Oct. 1, 8 years ago
Child: Zachary Nathan (6)
Employment History: 8 years with Miller & Miller, MU other employment
Education: B.S. degree in accounting, Ohio University, 13 years ago
No prior lawsuits
Incident date: Aug. 21, three months ago

Beginning two week vacation. Stopped first day at Maple Meadows Campground, site 36. As setting up camper, saw black electrical cord near where Zach was playing. Moved cord away from campsite. Cord was worn and rubber casing was broken in several spots. Plugged camper into extension cord that was taped to regular outlet. Noticed camper light and radio increasingly flickering off and on. Static on radio became quite loud. Heard son yell and emerged from camper to see son trapped by grass and brush fire. I grabbed old brown army blanket from camper and threw it around me. I ran through some flames to get to my son. I wrapped him in the blanket and carried him on my shoulder through the flames. I wore a short-sleeved shirt and khaki shorts, jogging shoes, no socks. Son was ok but my clothes were burning in several places. Zoe and I used another blanket to extinguish the flames burning my clothes and hair. I was obviously burned on my legs and arms. A maintenance worker at the camp took me to the hospital. Zoe and Zach followed in our car. Don't know worker's name.

Defendants: Camp owners Leroy and Margie Congden, Highway 60, Star Route 2, Legalville, Columbia. Their insurance carrier is Citizens Insurance Company of Hartford, Connecticut. They have not paid me anything, nor have I signed anything or made any statements to them.

Weather Conditions: dry and windy

Description of Campsite: MU

Statements: I told Dr. and nurses what happened. I have also told friends that I thought fire was caused by extension cord.

Witnesses: Mr. Robert Warren (in campsite 34) who is from Legalville and goes to campground occasionally on weekends. I do not have his address. I had spoken to him in afternoon after arrival. Told him of having electrical problems.

Medical: I suffered first-degree burns on my legs, hands, and left side of my face as well as numerous second- and third-degree burns. About 12 percent of my body was burned. Inhaled smoke but no serious damage to lungs. Felt nauseous and the burns were very painful. Hospitalized for two months. Had several skin graft operations. Doctors say I have significant permanent scars on face, hands, and legs.

Restrictions: Restricted movement of right (writing) hand. Some difficulty holding pencil. Overall movement still restricted. Doctors unsure whether restriction permanent or not. Hair beginning to grow back in most places. The pain is less now, but it was severe for the first month.

I still find the burn damage repulsive.

Hospital: Capitol County General Hospital, 400 Ridge Boulevard, Legalville

Treatment: Emergency treatment for burns Aug. 21, hospitalized 8/21–10/1

Surgery: Skin grafts to left cheek and left ankle by Albert Find, M.D., plastic surgeon, 313 Broad Street, Legalville

Prior Medical History: Healthy, broken ankle playing softball six years ago, normal childhood diseases

Damages: Employment, out of work since accident. May begin in approximately one month, but burn scars will make it hard to face clients.

Pain and Suffering (past-present-future) Estimate:

First month—terrible	$300/day
Second month	$200/day
Third month	$150/day

Rest of life because of scarring (embarrassment), some limitation in movement and use of hand—$40/day

Loss of Consortium (love and affection): 3 months at $50/day
Loss of Earnings: Out of work for 3 months

Scarring could cost 10% of clients

Medical:

Hospital Emergency Room	$3,000
61 days × 400/day	$24,000
Dr., surgery	$10,000
Prescriptions	$700

Other Property: Camper

and equipment	$2,000
Other: Loss of vacation	$1,000

4. Enter into a computer the notes from your interview with Mr. Ameche. Using a duplicate of these notes, delete extraneous material and organize the remaining important information into a summary according to the format in Exhibit 2:7.

Interview Summary Sheet

File No.   Date opened: Interviewer:
Client: Spouse: Children, ages:
Phone:
Date of injury: Statute of limitations:
Summary of facts of action:
Type of action:

Facts related to elements of action:
Facts related to possible defenses:
Witnesses:
Summary of injury and treatment to date:

Total medical bills to date:
Summary of business or wage loss:

Evaluation of client as witness:
Other comments:

Things to do:

---

5. Your firm is handling a wrongful death case for the plaintiff. Since the deceased is not available to testify, how can you introduce the human factor into the case? Who would you interview and what information would you want to gather? What information would you gather in other ways?

Now assume you work for the defense. What information would you gather and how would you gather it?

_____

_____

_____

_____

Internet Exercises

1.   Go to http://www.atanet.org, click on *find a translator*, and locate the name of an ATA certified translator for Japanese to English translation.

2.   Go to the ABA site in Helpful Web Sites. What is the title of the law practice periodical in which the article *Dealing with Difficult Clients* appears?

Additional Learning Exercises and Discussion Points

1.   List the essential elements and defenses to a cause of action for breach of contract.

_____

_____

_____

2.   Using the information following the sample interview form in the text, list the procedural stages for creating your own interview form and place it in your system folder.

_____

_____

_____

3.   Review the *Ameche* case (Case II). Prepare at least five interview questions that will elicit specific details of this nonautomobile accident.

_____

_____

_____

4.   Review the Checklist of Information to be given at the initial interview. Which three items do you think are most important? Explain.

_____

_____

_____

5.   Read the fee agreements in Exhibits 2:4 and 2:5. Briefly discuss the strengths and weaknesses of these agreements from the point of view of the firm, then from the point of view of the client.

_____

_____

_____

6.   How does the interviewer in the text example interview of Ms. Forrester demonstrate the criteria listed in Application Assignment 3?

_____

_____

_____

7.   One of the most common client complaints is, "My attorney never lets me know what is going on—and she (or he) is never available." Drawing from your text, in what specific ways can a paralegal assist the client in this regard?

_____

_____

_____

_____

8.   Work through the questions for study and review in the text to test your understanding of the chapter.

_____

_____

_____

Chapter Review Test and Answers

Review Test

Fill in the Blank

1. Sample interview forms and other forms can be found in _____, _____, and_____.
2. Good sources for researching the necessary elements of a cause of action are_____ and _____.
3. One element of negligence is that a breach of duty has to be the _____ of the injury.
4. Authorizations to release protected medical records must be _____ compliant.
5. One of the most frequent complaints of clients is _____.

True or False

T F 1.   Since each case is unique, interview form questions are not helpful.

T F 2.   Individuals have a duty not to create an unreasonable risk of harm to others.

T F 3.   Since toys are a distraction, do not keep them in the room when interviewing children.

T F 4.   In the interview, encourage the client to give all information about the accident, even if it is not in the client's favor.

T F 5.   Euphemisms are a good way to deal with sensitive issues in interviews.

T F 6.   Pace and lead is a technique used to elicit information during the client interview.

T F 7.   It is better to do a conflict of interest check after the client interview than before it.

Multiple Choice

1. A good interview form does all the following except:
   a. includes questions on employment background
   b. gives you all the questions you will need
   c. saves preparation time
   d. requires specific information on damages

2. Prominent signs declare a beach closed because of pollution. A swimmer who ignores the signs and later is hospitalized with an infection sues the owner of the beach. What defense does the owner have?
   a. breach of duty
   b. contributory negligence
   c. assumption of risk
   d. procedural law

3. The best way to record a client interview is to
   a. take notes
   b. tape record it
   c. have the client sign a written statement
   d. videotape it

4. Body language of a person may best be assessed to determine
   a. whether the person is lying
   b. that the person is confident
   c. how a jury will perceive the person
   d. a. and b.

5. Fee agreements
   a. are never discussed by paralegals
   b. are set by paralegals
   c. are always based on billable hours
   d. require the client's signature

6. What forms authorize doctors or others holding confidential information to give that information to a lawyer or paralegal?
   a. docket control forms
   b. authorization forms
   c. request forms
   d. medical information forms

7. Which is the best interview question?
   a. You stopped to look before you crossed the road, didn't you?
   b. Why didn't you pay more attention to traffic?
   c. Do you know what Statute CS §127 requires?
   d. How long did it take you to cross the road?

8. Professional ethics require of the paralegal
   a. your best legal advice to the client
   b. that you do not question the truth of what the client tells you
   c. confidentiality of client information
   d. no questions that would embarrass the client

9. In concluding the interview, be sure to
   a. have the client sign necessary documents
   b. have the client sign a statement
   c. avoid any conversation that is not pertinent to the case
   d. encourage the client to promote his/her side of the case among friends

10. The interview summary is helpful for
    a. publicizing the case
    b. quick review of facts
    c. evidence at trial
    d. keeping the client informed

11. A letter to a potential client making it absolutely clear that the firm is rejecting that person's representation is a
    a. deauthorization letter
    b. CAFA letter
    c. conflict letter
    d. disengagement letter

Chapter Two: The Initial Interview

Short Answer

1. The initial client interview is significant for what three reasons?

_____

_____

_____

2. Define substantive law and procedural law.

_____

_____

_____

3. What are the elements of negligence?

_____

_____

_____

4. How do you generate interview questions for specific cases?

_____

_____

_____

5. What are some considerations in choosing an interview site?

_____

_____

_____

6. Is the client going to be the one who is suing or being sued in a contingent fee agreement? Explain.

_____

_____

_____

7. In what two ways is the statute of limitations significant to any given lawsuit?

_____

_____

_____

8. What kinds of materials should the personal injury client bring to the interview?

_____

_____

_____

9. In order not to jeopardize their case, clients should not:

_____

_____

_____

10. How is the interview summary prepared?

_____

_____

_____

11. What are three ways you can help keep your client informed?

_____

_____

_____

Answers to Review Test

Fill in the Blank

1. the firm's files, trial practice manuals, the library
2. jury instructions, legal encyclopedias
3. proximate cause
4. HIPAA
5. lack of communication

True or False	*Multiple Choice*	
1. F	1. b	8. c
2. T	2. c	9. a
3. F	3. a	10. b
4. T	4. c	11. d
5. F	5. d	
6. F	6. b	
7. F	7. d	

Short Answer

1. Establishes client-firm relationship, establishes client-paralegal relationship, begins investigation.

2. Substantive law defines the duties owed by one person to another. Procedural law defines the steps that must be followed in a lawsuit.

3. Duty, breach of duty, injury, breach was cause of injury.

4. Consider what is needed to prove elements of substantive law.

5. Convenience, privacy, access to evidence.

6. The one suing. Must be likely to win damages to pay the attorney a percentage.

7. An action must be filed before the running of the statute or the right to sue is lost. Provides defense to otherwise valid action.

8. Information on employment, insurance, medical treatment, bills, etc.

9. Sign documents releasing others from liability, accept payment for damages, make statements to others about the case, file an accident report without attorney approval.

10. From interview notes and interview form. Would be easiest using computer editing.

11. Schedule regular client report letters, promptly respond to all client inquiries, acknowledge receipt of information and material sent to you from client.

 For additional resources, visit our Web site at **http://www.paralegal .delmar.cengage.com.**

Chapter 3. EVIDENCE AND INVESTIGATION

Chapter Objective

The purpose of this chapter is to provide the background information and techniques for conducting a sound investigation, as well as the opportunity to practice those techniques.

Outline

I.   Introduction

II. The Relationship of Evidence Law to Investigation
   A.   Introduction
   B.   Evidence in General
   C.   Admissible Evidence
   D.   Inadmissibility of Some Types of Relevant Evidence
      1.   Evidence Based on Prejudice, Confusion, or Delay
      2.   Character Evidence
      3.   Evidence of Habit or Routine Practice
      4.   Evidence of Offers to Compromise, Insurance, and Remedial Measures
      5.   Evidence of Past Sexual Conduct, Past Sexual Crimes
      6.   Illegally Obtained Evidence
   E.   Privileges
   F.   Evidence Admissible from a Party
   G.   Rules Regarding the Testimony of a Witness
      1.   Requirement of Firsthand Knowledge
      2.   Opinion
      3.   Expert Opinion
      4.   Evidence of Character and Conduct of a Witness
      5.   Prior Statements of a Witness
      6.   Capacity to Observe, Record, Recollect, or Narrate
      7.   Hearsay and Exceptions
   H.   Rules Regarding Physical Evidence and Authentication
   I.   Other Evidentiary Concepts
      1.   Judicial Notice
      2.   Stipulations
      3.   Burden of Proof
      4.   Presumption
   J.   Sources for Researching Evidence Law

III. Planning the Investigation
   A.   Introduction
   B.   Review the File and Other Available Information
   C.   Identify the Essential Elements of Proof
   D.   Identify What Facts Will Be Needed
   E.   Determine What Sources, Including Witnesses, May Provide Facts
      1.   Sources of Information and Evidence
      2.   Electronic Investigation and the Internet: Law and General Topic Research
   F.   Methods for Gathering Information or Evidence
   G.   Record the Investigation Plan
   H.   Consult with the Supervising Attorney

Define

Testimonial evidence

_____

_____

Documentary evidence

_____

_____

Real evidence

_____

_____

Demonstrative evidence

_____

_____

Chapter Three: Evidence and Investigation

Direct evidence

_____

_____

Circumstantial evidence

_____

_____

Admissible evidence

_____

_____

Relevance

_____

_____

Material

_____

_____

Probative value of evidence

_____

_____

Habit

_____

_____

Routine

_____

_____

Res gestae statements

_____

_____

Chain of custody

_____

_____

Best evidence rule

_____

_____

Judicial notice

_____

_____

Stipulation

_____

_____

Burden of proof

_____

_____

Affirmative defenses

_____

_____

Preponderance of the evidence

_____

_____

Clear and convincing evidence

_____

_____

Proof beyond reasonable doubt

_____

_____

Presumption

_____

_____

Discovery

_____

_____

Attorney's work product

_____

_____

Workbook Assignments and Exercises

System Folder Assignments

1.   List the purposes of investigation at the beginning of the investigation section of your system folder.

2.   Locate a copy of the Federal Rules of Evidence. Note how a photocopy of the table of contents for these rules can serve as a quick reference guide to evidence. You may choose to photocopy the table of contents to the rules of evidence and write the state equivalent next to each rule. Record whether evidence is admissible (A) or inadmissible (I). Place the reference guide in the investigation section of your system folder.

3.   Place an example of an investigation plan into your system folder.

4.   Read those Model Rules of Professional Conduct cited in this chapter. Also read FED. R. CIV. P. 26 (b) (3), "Trial Preparation: Materials," and the state equivalent. Draft a guide titled "Ethical Applications to Investigation" and write out a one- or two-word topic head for each applicable rule and cite it. Then place the guide in your system folder.

5.   Place copies of Exhibit 3:4, Request for Medical Records (Cover Letter); Exhibit 3:5, Authorization to Disclose Health Information (HIPAA); and Exhibit 3:8, Accident Scene Checklist, in your system folder. Add any suggestions from class lecture or discussion.

6.   Place a reference note in your system folder, including page numbers, to the techniques for locating witnesses and experts listed in this chapter.

7.   Place these items in your system folder: Checklist for Witness Interview, Witness Information Cover Sheet, and a brief description of how to create interview questions.

    Creating Interview Questions:

8.   Place a reference note in your system folder, including page numbers, to the techniques for conducting a witness interview stated in this chapter.

9. After class discussion, draft your own list of tips for taking and drafting an effective witness statement and place it in your system folder.

10. Place a reference note in your system folder, including page numbers, to the techniques for preserving evidence stated in this chapter.

Application Assignments

1.   The following is a list of possible evidence in Case I. Based on your understanding of the necessary elements in a negligence case from Chapter 2, the information in this chapter, and the rules of evidence for both the federal (F) and your state courts (S), indicate whether the listed items of evidence are admissible (A) or inadmissible (I). State any applicable reason and rule number.

Evidence	Fed	State	Reason	Rule(s)
Witness: "Mr. Hart is a good baseball player."	I	I	irrelevant	F401 S
1. Witness: "Mr. Hart smelled of beer."				
2. Bloody video of Ms. Forrester's hip repair				
3. Witness: "Mr. Hart is a cautious person."				
4. Routine practice of Mercury to check all brakes of vehicles				
5. Forrester's offer to Mercury to settle for $50,000				
6. Hart told wife he was too tired to be driving				
7. Forrester's letter to friend stating she didn't look for traffic				
8. Friend's opinion that signature on letter is Forrester's				
9. Doctor's testimony that van caused Forrester's injuries				
10. Independent evidence that van caused Forrester's injuries				
11. Testimony from Hart's minister that Hart is honest				
12. Independent evidence that doctor previously said falling on the ice was cause of injury				
13. Witness: "Mr. Forrester said, 'Hart was going fast.'"				
14. Witness at scene: "That van driver didn't even try to stop."				
15. Nearby service station attendant: "Hart said before accident, 'I'm going to scrape off that windshield.'"				
16. Mercury vehicle service log				
17. Relevant former testimony of unavailable witness				
18. Duplicate photograph of left front fender of van where authenticity of original in question				
19. Witness identification of bald tires from Hart's van with proper chain of custody				

2.   Following the steps and examples of planning an investigation as presented in this chapter, create an investigation plan for Case II. Develop the elements and facts to be proved, the sources, and the methods to be used in a format similar to that in Exhibit 3:3.

Possible to Prove or Acquire	Possible Source of Information	Method	Cost
Defendants			
Breach of Duty			
Conditions at Scene			
Plaintiff's Injuries			
Comparative Negligence			

3.   Citing the relevant Model Rules of Professional Conduct, what should you do under the following circumstances?

a.   You need to see one last critical witness who you are fairly sure will not speak with you if you tell the witness you are representing Ann Forrester. You arrive at the witness's apartment and she answers the door. What should you do?

_____
_____
_____
_____

b.   You are investigating a low profit case where your elderly client is trying to hang onto the only house and property she has ever had. Yet, to interview the key witness in the case will cost more than the case will bring to the firm. What should you do?

_____
_____
_____
_____

c.   Your firm is representing a federal judge in a civil suit. You have come to admire this judge and know that the firm believes he is a very valuable client. One night you are working with the judge on his case. There is a letter in the file that the judge received from a third party. The judge asks you to change one word in the letter because he knows that is what the party said he meant in the first place. The judge has offered you a terrific federal job at the close of this case. What would you do?

_____
_____
_____
_____

d.   As you are preparing a legal memo on a case for your supervising attorney, your fellow paralegal tells you not to deal with or cite two of the strongest cases against you because that is likely to help the other side—especially if they failed to find these cases. What should you do?

_____
_____
_____
_____

4.   Following the directions of your instructor and the procedure set out in this chapter of the text and Chapter 2 on interviewing, conduct an interview with Robert Warren, a witness to the incident in Case II. After the interview, prepare a witness statement according to the recommended procedures and tips covered in this chapter.

Your instructor has background information on Robert Warren that will be used to prepare the witness.

_____
_____
_____
_____

Internet Exercises

1.   Using http://www.uscourts.gov/rules/index.html, link to a copy of the federal rules of evidence. Find out whether the federal rules of evidence apply at preliminary examinations in criminal cases. State the applicable rule number and specific sub-paragraph letter and number.

2.   Go to http://www.cpsc.gov. Assume your client was badly burned after raising and lowering the hood on her White (brand name) lawn and garden tractor. Determine if any of these tractors were recalled for fuel leaks and, if recalled, in what months of what years the recalled tractors were sold.

3.   Using at least two different Web sites for locating people listed in Exhibit 3:2, see if you can locate your phone number by entering your name. Next, try to find a friend's name by entering only the phone number.

Additional Learning Exercises and Discussion Points

1.   Make a list of three possible items of relevant evidence in the *Ameche* case (Case II) and in the *Briar Patch Doll* case (Case IV). Indicate the fact of consequence for each item and whether that item would be direct or circumstantial evidence, and whether it would be testimonial, documentary, real, or demonstrative.

Ameche
EVIDENCE:
FACT:
TYPE:

EVIDENCE:
FACT:
TYPE:

EVIDENCE:
FACT:
TYPE:

Briar Patch Dolls
EVIDENCE:
FACT:
TYPE:

EVIDENCE:
FACT:
TYPE:

EVIDENCE:
FACT:
TYPE:

2.   What are the major requirements and limits of relevancy?

_____

_____

_____

_____

3.   Place a copy of Exhibit 3:4, Request for Medical Records (Cover Letter) in the Gathering Evidence: Medical Records subsection of your system folder.

_____

_____

_____

_____

4. What tools would you need—and for what purposes—to investigate the accident scene in Case II?

_____

_____

_____

_____

5. List three possible witnesses to interview in the *Coleman v. Make Tracks, Inc.* wrongful death case (Case III) and the focus of each interview.

_____

_____

_____

_____

6. Drawing on the section on conducting an interview, draft a checklist of considerations for conducting a witness interview and place it in your system folder.

_____

_____

_____

_____

7. Write five interview questions to Jason Hackett, friend of Sean Coleman, and the specific issues in Case III that they will probe.

_____

_____

_____

_____

8. List four methods for recording the statement of a witness and note advantages or disadvantages for each.

_____

_____

_____

_____

9. Make a list of leads for further investigation provided by the interview with Ms. Schnabel in the text or with Mr. Warren in Application Assignment 4.

_____

_____

_____

_____

10. Summarize either Ms. Schnabel's or Mr. Warren's statement to be included on the Witness Information Cover Sheet for the case file.

_____

_____

_____

_____

11. Draft a detailed checklist for preserving evidence and file it in your system folder.

_____

_____

_____

_____

12. Sketch the Forrester accident scene from the viewpoint of Ms. Schnabel.

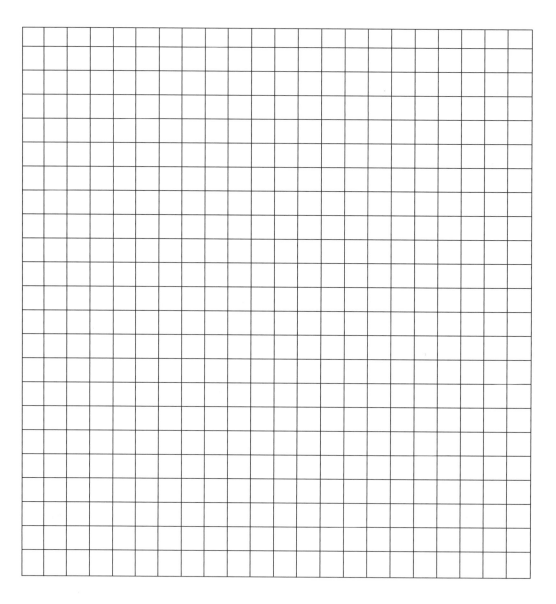

13. Work through the questions for study and review in the text to test your understanding of the chapter.

_____

_____

_____

_____

Chapter Review Test and Answers

Review Test

Fill in the Blank

1. The _____ of evidence must outweigh any prejudice, confusion, or delay it causes.
2. Physical evidence needs to be_____to be admissible.
3. Three levels of the burden of proof, from weakest to strongest, and the type of case to which they apply are

   _____, _____;

   _____, _____;

   _____, _____.

4. In the formal exchange of information, called _____the attorney's opinions and theories, called_____, are protected.
5. Items helpful in investigating an accident scene would include _____

   _____.

   _____.

6. Technical evidence may best be interpreted to a jury by _____.
7. The statements of witnesses who say they saw nothing can be used later to _____ _____them if they change their stories.
8. *Daubert v. Merrell Dow* (1993) confirmed the standard for admissibility of _____ _____.

9. Because of the perceived importance of prosecuting corporate fraud and controlling terrorism,_____privilege has come under significant erosive pressures.

True or False

T F 1.   The more evidence collected to prove a single point, the better.

T F 2.   Circumstantial evidence can be valuable to a case.

T F 3.   A chain of custody is a locking device used to prevent removal of valuable evidence.

T F 4.   You have no need to collect evidence that does not support your client's case.

T F 5.   A paralegal must identify position, employer, and purpose, even when speaking to unfriendly witnesses.

T F 6.   You should always answer the questions of a witness about a case.

T F 7.   It is best not to phone an evasive witness before you visit.

T F 8.   When drafting the statement of an uneducated witness, it is best to change the language to sound more sophisticated.

T F 9.   Once drafted, the witness statement should not be changed.

T F 10. A public relations expert is a good example of a third-party consultant to whom the attorney-client privilege might not apply.

Multiple Choice

1. To be admissible, evidence must be
   a. direct
   b. cumulative
   c. material
   d. privileged

2. Hearsay is admissible in the following except:
   a. res gestae statements
   b. quote from witness's conversation
   c. statement made to receive medical diagnosis
   d. statement of reputation

3. Self-authenticating evidence includes
   a. federal documents
   b. blood test results
   c. video tapes
   d. tire tread marks

4. Care in drafting an investigation plan is important because
   a. it must be authenticated by a judge
   b. it must conform to Rule 6(a)
   c. it is a record for billing
   d. it saves time and resources

5. Evidence is best gathered from key witnesses through a
   a. modem
   b. personal interview
   c. professional research service
   d. letter

6. Professional ethics require paralegals to
   a. make well-prepared statements to the press
   b. give loyalty to the client top priority
   c. refrain from obstructing opposition access to evidence
   d. ignore fraudulent behavior of clients if it is privileged

7. Important things to remember when requesting records include all except:
   a. keep the name of the client's physician's nurse on file
   b. narrative reports are often expensive
   c. information needs to be checked and corrected immediately
   d. follow-up letters are irritating to busy doctors and should be avoided

8. When interviewing witnesses
   a. ask questions that focus on elements of substantive law
   b. bring several together to save time
   c. don't worry about planning; go with your instincts
   d. never pay them a fee

9. A third party present at an interview can verify all except:
   a. that the witness read the statement
   b. that the witness statement is true
   c. that no improprieties occurred
   d. that the statement reflects the words of the witness

10. A well-drafted witness statement should
    a. be duplicated so the witness can have a copy
    b. note facts rather than beliefs
    c. should include names of all witnesses mentioned
    d. b and c

11. Sketches used as evidence should always
    a. be drawn to scale
    b. be keyed to photos being used
    c. be authenticated by a surveyor
    d. all of the above
    e. a and b

12. When you take physical evidence from a scene
    a. leave a receipt with your identity
    b. pay a fair price for it
    c. stamp or glue identification securely on it
    d. all of the above

13. A review of information from the informal investigation will help the attorney decide
    a. how much to charge the client
    b. what witnesses to have testify at trial
    c. whether to file a complaint
    d. whether to split the fee with the paralegal

14. HIPAA is the acronym for
    a. Health Information Portability and Accounting Act
    b. Health Information Privacy and Accountability Administration
    c. Health Insurance Portability and Accountability Act
    d. Health Insurance Privacy and Administration Act

15. HIPAA preempts
    a. less protective state law
    b. no state laws
    c. all state laws
    d. more protective state law

Short Answer

1. What is investigation? What are some components of informal investigation?

_____

_____

_____

2. List four types of evidence and an example of each.

_____

_____

_____

3. Why is evidence of habit or routine generally admissible?

_____

_____

_____

4. What is the difference between judicial notice and stipulation?

_____

_____

_____

5. List in order at least four of the steps in planning an investigation? Why is that plan important?

_____

_____

_____

6. Briefly outline the procedure for requesting reports, records, and other documents.

_____

_____

_____

7. Write a list of things to remember when requesting employment and financial information.

_____

_____

_____

8. What should you look for when you receive a reply to your request for records?

_____

_____

_____

9. Why is it helpful to investigate an accident scene at the same time of week and day as the accident occurred?

_____

_____

_____

10. Give two reasons for contacting witnesses early.

_____

_____

_____

11. What are three ways to find an unknown jogger who may have witnessed your client's accident?

_____

_____

_____

12. List three ways a witness statement can be useful to a case.

_____

_____

_____

13. Why should great care be taken with the wording of a witness statement? The initialing and signing of a witness statement?

_____

_____

_____

14. How do you decide which view of a scene is best for sketches or photos?

_____

_____

_____

15. Why is it necessary to preserve evidence in its discovered state?

_____

_____

_____

16. Briefly state when the duty to preserve electronic information begins and what is required by the duty.

_____

_____

_____

Answers to Review Test

Fill in the Blank

1. probative value
2. authenticated
3. preponderance of evidence, civil;
   clear and convincing evidence, special civil cases (fraud);
   proof beyond reasonable doubt, criminal
4. discovery, attorney's work product or trial preparation materials
5. measuring devices, camera, recorder, compass, stop watch, tags, bags, flashlight, magnifying glass, protractor, etc.
6. an expert witness
7. impeach
8. expert opinion
9. attorney-client

True or False		*Multiple Choice*	
1. F	8. F	1. c	9. b
2. T	9. F	2. b	10. b
3. F	10. T	3. a	11. e
4. F		4. d	12. a
5. T		5. b	13. c
6. F		6. c	14. c
7. T		7. d	15. a
		8. a	

Short Answer

1. The informal and formal gathering of information to determine facts in a case. Interviewing clients and witnesses. Reviewing documents, records, physical evidence, test results.

2. Testimonial—witness statement
   Documentary—business records
   Real—defective product
   Demonstrative—photo of scene of accident

3. Their invariable regularity and frequency make them valid and reliable.

4. Judicial notice permits judge to allow evidence without authentication. Stipulation permits an agreement between parties to allow evidence without authentication.

5. 1. Review file and information.
   2. Identify elements of proof.
   3. Identify facts to prove elements.
   4. Determine sources for facts.
   5. Record investigative plan.
   6. Consult with attorney.
   The plan helps make efficient use of time and resources for effective results.

6. Be sure client has signed current authorization.
   Call records custodian for fees, procedures, etc.
   Send letter properly identifying persons, dates, and specific information needed.
   Attach signed release and fee.

7. 1. Have client sign release of employment information at initial interview to include with request.
   2. Request brief history of annual earnings,
       current salary or hourly wage,
       days of work missed since accident,
       overtime and bonuses missed,
       disability insurance coverage.

8. Check that information is correct and clear.
   Check that vernacular can be deciphered.
   Request corrections or explanations immediately.

9. To observe traffic patterns, light, possible witnesses.

10. 1. They forget details with time.
    2. They tend to form attachments to first side who contacts them.

11. Newspaper ad, canvass neighborhood, review photos, visit accident scene at same time, ask local running groups.

12. 1. Tells the attorney what facts can be corroborated or refuted. (Reveals strengths and weaknesses of case.)
    2. Serves as record of witness's recollection of facts.

    —Used later to refresh memory of witness
    —Used later to impeach witness

    3. May help settle case.

13. Wording could indicate uncertainty or inaccuracies.
    Initialing and signing are verification of statement.

14. Look for clarity on depicting the event and point of view of parties and witnesses. Show significant features and relationships.

15. Any changes may obscure the facts of the event, result in unprofessional conduct charges against you or the attorney.

16. The duty is invoked by statute, or when the party first knew or should have known that the evidence is potentially relevant to litigation. The party must prevent destruction and corruption of the evidence.

 For additional resources, visit our Web site at **http://www.paralegal .delmar.cengage.com.**

Chapter 4. DRAFTING THE COMPLAINT

Chapter Objective

This chapter helps you develop the knowledge, skills, and techniques needed to draft the complaint for a civil lawsuit and gain experience in drafting complaints.

Outline

Define

Due process of law

_____

_____

Pleadings

_____

_____

Complaint

_____

_____

Plaintiff

_____

_____

Defendant

_____

_____

Real party in interest

_____

_____

Standing to sue

_____

_____

Capacity

_____

_____

Guardian ad litem

_____

_____

Joinder of parties

_____

_____

Interpleader

_____

_____

Class action

_____

_____

Cause of action

_____

_____

Fact pleading

_____

_____

Notice pleading

_____

_____

General damages

_____

_____

Special damages

_____

_____

Exemplary (punitive) damages

_____

_____

Prohibitory injunction

_____

_____

Mandatory injunction

_____

_____

Specific performance

_____

_____

Workbook Assignments and Exercises

System Folder Assignments

1.   Research the rules of civil procedure for your state for the recommended caption form. If the rules of your state do not have sample forms, go to a book on forms for civil action in your state. Place a copy of the state caption form with copies of the captions from the text at the beginning of the complaint section of your system folder. Also list the applicable rules and forms. Note any state rules or policy regarding the redaction of privacy information.

2.   Following class discussion on drafting complaints, especially regarding state court rules, complete the state and system folder reference blanks in the System Checklist for Drafting a Complaint, and place it in your system folder.

3.   Check the pleading rules of your own state. Gather examples of local complaints by researching recent editions of legal forms and pleading books, or obtain them from your instructor. Try to locate a full range of examples of complaints that include pleading in the alternative, pleading in the hypothetical, joined parties, and joined claims and counts. Place them in your system folder. Add references to the page numbers in this text where samples of specific types of complaints can be located. Add references to or copies of injunction and restraining order forms.

Application Assignments

1.   Should an insurance company have to pay exemplary damages on behalf of the insured? State arguments for and against.

_____

_____

_____

_____

2. Using the checklist and examples in the text, draft a complaint for Ann Forrester to be filed in the United States District Court for the Eastern District of Columbia alleging diversity jurisdiction. Place copies of the federal (notice) complaint and the state (fact) complaint into your system folder.

Federal Notice Complaint for *Ann Forrester* Case

_____

_____

_____

_____

3. Draft both a fact and a notice complaint for the *Ameche* case (Case II in Chapter 1) using the facts you found through investigation in Chapter 3.

_____

_____

_____

_____

Internet Exercises

1. Go to http://www.ojp.usdoj.gov/bjs/civil.htm. Under BJS Publications, click on Federal Tort Trials and Verdicts, 2002–03. In 2002–2003, what percentage of tort cases went to trial? What percentage of federal cases was based on diversity jurisdiction?

2. A previous edition of this text stated that Alabama had a law requiring that punitive damages over a certain amount be split with the state. Using Westlaw, Lexis, or a lawfinder such as http://www.lawresearch.com, go to state materials and then the state statutes of Alabama. Using the index to the statutes or a search box, find out if that is still the law in Alabama.

Additional Learning Exercises and Discussion Points

1. a. What is a syllogism and what are its components?

_____

_____

_____

    b. In your own words, explain a cause of action for negligence in terms of a syllogism.

_____

_____

_____

2. List the five suggested references on good legal writing and add them to your system folder.

_____

_____

_____

3. What are the federal court privacy restrictions governing redactions of Social Security numbers, names of minors, birth dates, and addresses? What federal rule governs this after December 2007?

_____

_____

_____

4.   What Federal Rules of Civil Procedure cover notice pleading requirements? Compare and contrast fact (code) pleading with notice pleading.

_____
_____
_____

5.   What 2003 U.S. Supreme Court case reaffirmed the principle that punitive damages must be reasonable to be constitutional? What is the constitutional concept applied, and what key factors determine reasonability of punitives?

_____
_____
_____

6.   List and give examples of four types of remedies typically sought by plaintiffs in civil litigation.

_____
_____
_____

7.   Using the text guide to causes of actions and remedies, write the cause of action and wherefore clause (with an example of at least one type of remedy available) for a complaint in each of the following fact situations. Then state whether the syllogism is complete; that is, whether all elements are present, or what elements are lacking, to state a cause of action upon which relief may be granted.

    a.   Alice Jones has been transferred and must move by May 1. On her realtor's advice and in order to help sell her home, she hires Elegance Interiors to redecorate it. Elegance contracts to complete the work by March 1 and accepts payment for materials from Jones. On February 20, Elegance returns the money and notifies Jones that another obligation prevents work on her house until April 16. Jones sues for anticipatory breach of contract.

_____
_____
_____

    b.   Micky Speer has contracted with hall of fame trainer Eddie Fast to train Mr. Fix, a racehorse, for the Kentucky Derby. Fast resigns on April 6, ___, a month before the race, in a dispute over fringe benefits. To force Fast to train his horse through the race of a lifetime, Speer sues for specific performance.

_____
_____
_____

    c.   Sleepy Time Motel manager Edna Bains resigns and uses an inheritance to buy the Tick Tock Inn down the street. The manager of Overroad Trucking, whose drivers always stay at Sleepy Time, shows the owners of Sleepy Time a letter from Bains offering Overroad a discount for staying at Tick Tock and referring to Sleepy Time as a dump. Sleepy Time sues for tortious interference with prospective economic advantage.

_____
_____
_____

8.   Work through the questions for study and review at the end of Chapter 4 in the text to test your understanding of the chapter.

_____
_____
_____

Chapter Review Test and Answers

Review Test

Fill in the Blank

1. Due process of law is guaranteed in the _____ and _____ Amendments of the Constitution.

2. The caption of a complaint includes _____, and sometimes _____.

3. Standing to sue is granted only to those who_____ _____.

4. Rule_____ of the Federal Rules of Procedure designates what must be included in a pleading filed in federal court.

5. All pleadings except_____ may use the abbreviation _____ after the first name, rather than list multiple parties.

6. A logical formula for an argument is a _____.

7. Documents filed to require a party to do or refrain from doing some act are_____ and _____.

8. Due process requires that exemplary (punitive) damages must be _____.

True or False

T F 1.   When filing a complaint or other document electronically, the signature should also include the statement "electronically filed."

T F 2.   A complaint is the formal introduction of a lawsuit.

T F 3.   Ms. Schnabel is a real party in interest in the *Forrester* case.

T F 4.   Jurisdictional amount must be alleged in federal question complaints.

T F 5.   Briar Patch Dolls (Case IV) does most of its business in Colombia, where Teeny Tiny Manufacturing is located, but federal diversity exists because Briar Patch is incorporated in Ohio.

T F 6.   It's best to avoid the archaic language found in some legal forms when you draft documents.

Multiple Choice

1. A poorly drafted complaint can cause all the following except:
   a. delay
   b. injunction
   c. negative impressions
   d. dismissal

Chapter Four: Drafting the Complaint

2. Pleadings include
   a. cross claims
   b. memoranda
   c. motions
   d. evidence

3. What is required for ability to sue or be sued?
   a. capacity
   b. domicile
   c. real party in interest
   d. a and c
   e. all of the above

4. A guardian ad litem permits suit when
   a. a corporation is a party
   b. there is no interpleader
   c. there is a lack of capacity
   d. multiple parties are joined

5. Requirements for class action suits include all except:
   a. action of the adverse party is inconsistent toward members of the class
   b. members of the class are too numerous for joinder
   c. the representative will protect the interests of the class
   d. there are common questions of law and fact

6. Language in the complaint needs to
   a. prove the plaintiff's case
   b. be assertive
   c. address possible defenses
   d. state the law

7. Adequately stating a cause of action in a particular jurisdiction requires research into all except:
   a. local court rules of procedure
   b. case law applicable to that court
   c. Federal Rules of Civil Procedure
   d. successful pleadings previously filed in that court

8. Fact (code) pleading
   a. is used in federal courts
   b. is simple and requires no technical forms
   c. is used in all state courts
   d. must support each element of the rule of law

9. Money sought as punishment for malicious conduct is
   a. special damages
   b. specific performance
   c. exemplary damages
   d. prohibitory injunctions

10. A wherefore clause states
    a. the demand for relief
    b. the cause of action
    c. the elements of law
    d. the counterclaim

11. Demand for jury trial should
    a. be postponed until beginning of trial
    b. be made within 30 days of service of the last pleading
    c. always be included in the complaint
    d. be conspicuous

12. Appendices to complaints usually include
    a. contracts
    b. explanatory material
    c. bills of lading
    d. motions to dismiss

13. In filing legal documents, procedures regarding protection of personal privacy information are determined by
    a. the ABA rules on e-filing
    b. the format chosen by the opponent
    c. the attorney filing the document
    d. federal court policy

14. Pain and suffering and emotional distress are included in
    a. mandatory damages
    b. noneconomic damages
    c. exemplary damages
    d. special damages

Short Answer

1. What do pleadings have to do with our right to due process?

_____
_____
_____
_____

2. a.   Why can the caption of Case IV read *Briar Patch Dolls, Inc. v. Teeny Tiny Manufacturing Co.* rather than *Heinz v. Smith and McGinnis*?

_____
_____
_____

   b.   If Teeny Tiny were owned solely by Ethel Meyers, now deceased, could Briar Patch still sue? Why?

_____
_____
_____

3. List four ways that related claims are handled to save costs and time, and their pertinent Federal Rules of Civil Procedure.

_____
_____
_____

4. What information must be presented to allege jurisdiction in a state court?

_____
_____
_____

5. Why must jurisdiction always be alleged in federal courts but not all state courts?

_____

_____

_____

6. Why does venue not have to be alleged in complaints in federal court?

_____

_____

_____

7. How are separate claims stated in a complaint?

_____

_____

_____

8. Why is it necessary to research local practice in drafting complaints in a particular state jurisdiction?

_____

_____

_____

9. Why are the subscription and verification of a complaint important?

_____

_____

_____

10. What other documents might be attached to a complaint and for what purposes?

_____

_____

_____

11. What does it mean to say in a pleading, "Incorporate by reference paragraph 2 of Count One"?

_____

_____

_____

Answers to Review Test

Fill in the Blanks

1. 5th, 14th
2. the name and location of the court, file number, parties, nature of the action
3. have suffered or will suffer a direct or actual injury
4. 10
5. the complaint, et al.
6. syllogism
7. preliminary injunctions, temporary restraining order
8. reasonable

True or False		*Multiple Choice*		
1. F		1. b	7. c	13. d
2. T		2. a	8. d	14. b
3. F		3. d	9. c	
4. F		4. c	10. a	
5. F		5. a	11. d	
6. T		6. b	12. b	

Short Answer

1. Pleadings clarify issues and inform parties of the basis for claims or defenses, keeping the litigation procedure open and fair; we cannot be deprived of property without the opportunity to defend our property.

2. a.   Corporations are considered persons.

    The contract was between corporations, not individuals.

   b.   Yes. Her estate would be responsible for her legal obligations.

3. 1.   Joinder of parties—Rules 19(a) and 20(a)
   2.   Interpleader rule—Rule 22
   3.   Class actions—Rule 23
   4.   Motion to intervene—Rule 24(c)

4. Names and domiciles of parties
   Cause of action and its location
   Reference to controlling state statute on jurisdiction
   Any jurisdictional amount

5. Federal courts are courts of limited subject matter jurisdiction, so jurisdiction must be demonstrated. State trial courts are courts of general jurisdiction, meaning they will hear almost everything.

6. Venue is considered a matter for defendant to raise; may be waived.

7. In separate counts, each having its own body of allegations, damages, and demand for judgment; and incorporating common information from introductory paragraphs.

8. Pleading rules and procedures vary from one jurisdiction to another. If the complaint is inadequate, it may be dismissed or have to be amended.

9. By signing the document, both attorney (subscription) and party (verification) attest to the truth and validity of the claim; deters the filing of false claims.

10. Verification or certification—statement by party on truth of complaint, exhibits—documents at issue, and appendices—explanation of language, etc.

11. Read section as if paragraph 2 of Count One of the pleading is restated at this point. Makes it unnecessary to repeat language.

  For additional resources, visit our Web site at **http://www.paralegal .delmar.cengage.com.**

Chapter 5. FILING THE LAWSUIT, SERVICE OF PROCESS, AND OBTAINING THE DEFAULT JUDGMENT

Chapter Objective

The purpose of this chapter is to enable you to file an action properly, effect service of the summons and complaint on the defendant, and draft documents required to obtain a default judgment. You will practice working with applicable rules of civil procedure for both the state and federal systems, as well as with the documents required by each.

Outline

I. Introduction
    A. The Tasks: Filing the Lawsuit, Serving the Summons, Obtaining a Default Judgment
    B. Purpose of the Tasks

II. Preparing Documents for Filing an Action and for Service of Process
    A. Determine What Documents Are Needed
    B. Gather and Prepare the Documents Necessary for Filing and Service
        1. Introduction
        2. Complaint
        3. Summons
        4. Civil Cover Sheet
        5. Notice of Lawsuit and Request for Waiver of Service of Summons; Waiver of Service of Summons
        6. Request for Service of Process
        7. Motion for Special Appointment to Serve Process
        8. Affidavit of Service of Summons and Complaint
        9. Consent to Exercise of Jurisdiction by Magistrate Judge
        10. Nongovernmental Corporation Disclosure Statement
    C. Obtain the Check for the Filing Fees

III. Filing the Lawsuit
    A. Traditional Methods of Filing
    B. E-Filing

IV. Service of Process

V. Reference Guide and Checklist for Methods of Service
    A. Service on Individuals in a State or in a Judicial District of the United States
    B. Service on Individuals in a Foreign Country [Rule 4(f)]
    C. Service on Corporations and Associations [Rule 4(h)]
    D. Service on the United States [Rule 4(i)]
    E. Service on a Foreign, State, or Local Government
    F. Service Outside the Geographical Boundaries of the State or Federal District Court/Long-Arm Statutes
    G. Service in In Rem and Quasi In Rem Cases
    H. Immunity from Service of Process

Define

Service of process

_____

_____

Summons

_____

_____

In forma pauperis

_____

_____

Long-arm statute

_____

_____

In rem action

_____

_____

Quasi in rem

_____

_____

Constructive service

_____

_____

Substituted service

_____

_____

Default judgment

_____

_____

Workbook Assignments and Exercises

System Folder Assignments

1.   Obtain fee schedules for the federal, state, and local courts, including fees for service of process and the person to whom such service fees should be paid, as well as fees for the filing of subsequent pleadings and motions. If so directed by your instructor, contact the

appropriate clerk of court for this information. Place the fee schedules in your system folder with a reminder to update the information periodically.

2.   Place a copy of Exhibit 5:9, Checklist for E-Filings, in your system folder.

3.   Using an approach similar to the Reference Guide and Checklist for Methods of Service, draft a state service of process checklist for your system folder. Look up any needed information in your state's rules of civil procedure or state statutes to complete your checklist.

4.   After class discussion on locating difficult-to-find defendants, add additional techniques to the Checklist for Locating Defendants. Place the checklist in your system folder.

5.   Draft a brief Checklist for Filing and Service of Documents Subsequent to the Complaint—Federal and a similar one for your state. Note the applicable rules for future reference including any on e-filing and service. Place the checklists in your system folder.

6.   In your system folder make a reference to the checklist for default judgment. Research the rules and forms applicable to obtaining a default judgment in your state courts, and draft a state checklist for default judgment. Add needed state forms to your system folder.

7.   Refer to the motion to set aside default judgment and the notice of motion in your system folder.

8.   Your system folder should have a guide to both federal and state time limits. Two rules in this chapter give specific time limits that must be met. They are Rule 55(b)(2), which requires that notice of a hearing on an application for default judgment be served on the defendant or representative at least three days prior to the hearing, and Rule 60(b), which requires a motion to set aside a default judgment to be filed within one year from the date of the judgment in specified circumstances. Keeping track of time requirements and calendaring them is extremely important. See the Pleadings, Motions, and Time Limits table in Chapter 6. Verify both state and federal deadlines for default judgments and all other deadlines as they arise.

Application Assignments

1.   Prepare the necessary documents for filing Case II, the *Ameche* case, for both federal and your state courts. Use the sample forms provided in this chapter and the completed forms as a guide. Assume there is diversity jurisdiction. Check for accuracy. Place these samples of your work and page references to the forms in this text in your system folder.

_____
_____
_____
_____

2.

Memo to: Terry Salyer, Paralegal

From: Isadora Pearlman

Subject: Research

Completion Date: Three days from today

Issue: What are the necessary minimum contacts required by our state statute to gain jurisdiction over a foreign corporation? Over a nonresident tort feasor? Over an Internet marketer?

Task: Prepare a short memorandum on the state and constitutional law on this subject.

Guidelines: Check the annotated state statutes under "long-arm statutes," "foreign corporations," and "non-resident tort feasors" for case law. Also try the state digest under similar key phrases. Since the state's long-arm statute affects both our federal and state court, decisions in both jurisdictions are helpful. See the section on researching and drafting a memorandum of law in Chapter 6.

---

3.   Assume for purposes of this assignment that Mr. Hart is an incompetent person; that he is the only defendant in the *Ann Forrester* case; that Mr. Hart's guardian has been served with a summons and complaint; and that the guardian did not respond within the required 20 days. Draft the necessary state documents to obtain a default judgment in the case. Use your checklist.

_____

_____

_____

_____

4.   Assume that you work for the firm that is representing Richard Hart and that for purposes of this problem, Mr. Hart is elderly and not well educated. He comes to your firm six months after a default judgment has been entered against him. Your attorney assigns you the task of determining if limited capacity brought on by aging and lack of education is sufficient good cause to have a default judgment set aside. Research the issue and prepare a brief outline on what facts are sufficient good cause to set aside a default judgment.

_____

_____

_____

_____

Internet Exercises

1.   Go to http://www.uscourts.gov, click on Electronic Access to Courts, click on Case Management/Electronic Case Files Project, click on Court Links, then click on the links to your federal district court. Explore the site for free tutorials and materials on the CM/ECF system. Work through the online tutorial. If your court does not have a tutorial, link to one that does.

2.   Go to http://www.vedderprice.com. Search News and Publications Archive for the October 2003 article "Long-Arm Statutes: A Fifty-State Survey." In that article, find the case that illustrates Kansas law on out-of-state service of process in Internet cases.

3.   Assume you have hit a dead end trying to locate the defendant in your client's lawsuit. Your client is willing to pay only a small amount to continue the search. Go to the people locator sites listed in Helpful Web Sites and compare fees. What will the company charge if the search is not successful?

Additional Learning Exercises and Discussion Points

1.   Research your state counterpart to Rule 4(a) of the Federal Rules of Civil Procedure. Identify the number of the state rule and prepare a concise list of the content requirements for a valid summons in your state court. Place this in your system folder.

_____
_____
_____

2.   Outline the procedure for service of summons in your state. Are there special forms for request of service?

_____
_____
_____

3.   Go to the Web site for your state courts and determine if any levels of your state courts permit e-filing. If there is an e-filing system, what is its name? If not, are there plans to implement an e-system? Is there a tutorial for its use? How does an attorney access and use the system?

_____
_____
_____

4.   Outline the process of filing the lawsuit.

_____
_____
_____

5.   Who is usually immune from service of process? Speculate on why this is so.

_____
_____
_____

6.   Research Section 804 of the Federal Debt Collections Practices Act. Which of the following practices would be unlawful in trying to locate a defendant?
   a.   A paralegal contacts a neighbor of the defendant to locate the defendant.
   b.   A paralegal informs a third person that the paralegal is a debt collector.
   c.   A paralegal informs a third party that the defendant owes the plaintiff money after third party asks, "Does the defendant owe you money?"
   Does your state have similar rules? Research them and describe them here. Do you believe these restrictions are wise?

_____
_____
_____

7.   Consider grounds for setting aside a default judgment, then speculate on why an affidavit of nonmilitary service of defendant is required in most jurisdictions.

_____
_____
_____

8.   Research your state statutes and pertinent cases to determine the most common factual situations that are sufficient to set aside a default judgment. According to the law, what should the court consider in determining whether a default judgment should be set aside?

_____
_____

_____

9.   Work through the questions for study and review at the end of Chapter 5 in the text to test your understanding of the chapter.

_____
_____
_____

Chapter Review Test and Answers

Review Test

Fill in the Blank

1. A good Web site for federal court rules and forms is _____.

2. The first formal step in the litigation process is _____
   _____.

3. _____is the document that gives the defendant the time within
   which to appear and defend.

4. Typical long-arm statutes require service of process through _____
   _____.

5. Federal rules require the summons and complaint to be served on the defendant
   within_____ of the filing of the complaint.

6. In default judgments a monetary amount not readily challengeable or subject to
   reasonable dispute is called _____.

7. The Service Members Civil Relief Act gives service personnel _____ days after release
   from active duty to reopen a default judgment.

True or False

T F 1. Case deadlines in an action stem from the filing of the request for service of
process.

T F 2. Documents to file a lawsuit must be delivered to the clerk of court in person.

T F 3. A benefit of court e-filing systems is accessibility from outside the law office.

T F 4. Following traditional service of the summons and obtaining proper consent,
subsequent documents may be filed electronically.

T F 5. In serving an officer of the United States, service is complete simply by serving a
copy of the summons and complaint on the U.S. Attorney General.

T F 6. A one-year statute of limitations and the need of an injured party to first file an
administrative claim applies to the Federal Tort Claims Act.

T F 7. Constructive service is most often used in in rem actions.

T F 8. The Freedom of Information Act may be helpful in finding the address
of a defendant.

T F 9. Default judgments may award amounts greater than those requested in the complaint.

Multiple Choice

1. A nongovernmental corporation must disclose any parent corporation
   a. on its first appearance in the case
   b. as soon as discovery is complete
   c. as a response to a motion by the opposing party
   d. any time before trial

2. Service of process
   a. is necessary before a default judgment can be entered
   b. establishes personal jurisdiction
   c. officially notifies the defendant of the lawsuit
   d. all of the above

3. The best source for finding out for the first time what documents are needed in a state court is
   a. your system checklist
   b. the clerk of court
   c. another paralegal
   d. a reference book of forms

4. The Process Receipt and Return form must be filed when service of process is by
   a. U.S. marshal
   b. county sheriff
   c. secretary of state
   d. local constable

5. Notice of lawsuit and Request for Waiver of Service of Summons
   a. is designed to save time but not cost
   b. also requires a Waiver of Service of Summons
   c. also requires a copy of the original summons
   d. shortens the time to answer the complaint

6. Public access to federal court documents in specific cases is available through
   a. CM/ECF
   b. NEF
   c. PACER
   d. us.gov

7. Long-arm statutes allow service of process on out-of-state defendants as long as
   a. the defendant is a corporation
   b. service is by a U.S. marshal
   c. the defendant has had sufficient contacts with the state
   d. the plaintiff is also out-of-state

8. All the following may be immune from service of process except:
   a. witnesses attending trial
   b. agents of the United States
   c. defendants brought into a state by force
   d. defendants traveling to a trial

9. Service of papers subsequent to the complaint
   a. is covered in Rule 5 of the Federal Rules of Civil Procedure
   b. is directly on the party, not the party's attorney
   c. must be preceded by filing them with the clerk of court
   d. all of the above
   e. a and b

10. A request for entry of default judgment is often accompanied by an affidavit to show
    a. amount due
    b. incapacity of defendant
    c. nonmilitary service
    d. waiver of service of summons

11. A hearing on an application for default judgment requires
    a. no special preparation
    b. evidence to prove amount of damages
    c. 20 days' notice
    d. defendant's testimony

12. Good cause to set aside a default judgment includes all except:
    a. illness of defendant's attorney
    b. the judgment has been satisfied
    c. the amount of damages requested is unfair
    d. misconduct of adverse party

Short Answer

1. Why is it important to confirm the method of service of process with the attorney before filing?

   _____
   _____
   _____

2. Generally, when does an action officially begin in state court and in federal court?

   _____
   _____
   _____

3. What does the clerk of court do in filing a case?

   _____
   _____
   _____

4. Identify and give the significance of NEF.

   _____
   _____
   _____

5. How is federal service of an in-state corporation accomplished?

   _____
   _____
   _____

6. Compare in rem and quasi in rem actions.

   _____
   _____
   _____

7. What cautions should be observed in locating defendants?

   _____
   _____
   _____

8. What is the difference between the entry of default and the entry of default judgment?

   _____
   _____
   _____

9. To whom is the request for entry of default judgment submitted?

_____

_____

_____

10. What cautions apply when seeking default judgments against multiple defendants?

_____

_____

_____

11. What time limits are involved in setting aside a default judgment?

_____

_____

_____

Answers to Review Test

Fill in the Blank

1. www.uscourts.gov
2. filing the complaint
3. The summons
4. the secretary of state
5. 120 days
6. sum certain
7. 90

True or False	Multiple Choice	
1. F	1. a	8. b
2. F	2. d	9. a
3. T	3. b	10. e
4. T	4. a	11. b
5. F	5. b	12. c
6. F	6. c	
7. F	7. c	
8. T		
9. F		

Short Answer

1. Documents delivered to the clerk of court for filing may be different for different types of service.

2. State court—when complaint and summons are served on defendant. Federal court—when complaint is delivered to the clerk of court.

3. Dates original complaint
    Assigns a civil case number
    Possibly assigns judge
    Issues summons
    Checks summons and civil cover sheet

4. NEF is the automatic Notice of Electronic Filing in the federal system. It provides instant confirmation of an electronic filing, notice to the other parties, and constitutes service.

5. a. If no waiver is obtained, according to law of state in which the pertinent district court is located, *or*
    b. serve an officer, general agent, or any other agent authorized by law or appointment to receive service (often secretary of state)
    c. and, if statute requires, mail copy to defendant [Rule 4(C)(1 or 2)]

6. Both involve the attachment of property.
    in rem, to resolve claims to the property itself;
    quasi in rem, to pay a judgment in an unrelated case where personal jurisdiction has not been established over the defendant.

7. Federal Collections Act and local laws to avoid harassment or illegal collection practices.

8. Entry of default establishes the time of the default after which defendant generally cannot contest liability. Entry of default judgment determines plaintiff's victory and remedy.

9. To the clerk if award is sum certain, to the court if the award is yet to be determined.

10. Some jurisdictions allow only one judgment, precluding action against other defendants. Other jurisdictions allow designating the judgment as joint and several.

11. Motion must be made in reasonable time (up to a year from judgment for Rule 60(b)(1-3). Notice of a hearing on an application for default judgment must be served on the defendant or representative at least three days prior to the hearing (Rule 55(b)(2)). If successful, answer can be filed as if time limit had not expired.

 For additional resources, visit our Web site at **http://www.paralegal .delmar.cengage.com.**

Chapter 6. DEFENDING AND TESTING THE LAWSUIT: MOTIONS, ANSWERS, AND OTHER RESPONSIVE PLEADINGS

Chapter Objective

This chapter aims to familiarize you with the variety of pleadings and procedures that will follow service of the complaint. It covers motions in general and motions to dismiss; removal to federal court; the answer, counterclaim and cross-claim; motion on the pleadings; amendments to the pleadings; and summary judgment.

Outline

Define

Motion

_____

_____

Order

_____

_____

Memorandum of law

_____

_____

Brief

_____

_____

Affidavit

_____

_____

Affiant

_____

_____

Demurrer

_____

_____

Bill of particulars
_____
_____

Answer
_____
_____

Argumentative denials
_____
_____

Counterclaim
_____
_____

Cross-claim
_____
_____

Third-party practice (impleader)
_____
_____

Workbook Assignments and Exercises

System Folder Assignments

1.   Locate in your state rules the requirements, procedures, and time limits that apply to motions. Write a checklist for drafting, filing, and serving motions for both state and federal court, and place it in your system folder. Verify the time limits pertaining to motions in the Pleadings, Motions, and Time Limits table at the end of the chapter. Add state deadlines.

2.   Make references in your system folder to the documents in this text needed to file a motion to dismiss the complaint. Add any pertinent state practice forms.

3.   Place page references to or copies of the Motion to Strike and the Motion to Make More Definite and Certain in your system folder.

4.   Enter a reference to or copy of the notice of removal to federal court in your system folder. Develop your own brief checklist for the required procedural stages and place that in your system folder.

5.   Note the rules for calculating time for both the federal and your state jurisdiction [see Rule 6(a) and (e)] in your system folder. Include the formula and the example on how to calculate the due date.

6.   Place a page reference to or copy of the list of style and content suggestions for the answer in your system folder.

7.   Add Exhibit 6:10, Forms of Denial in Pleadings, to your system folder, or enter a page reference to it.

8.   Place in your system folder a page reference to the steps in locating affirmative defenses.

9.   Place copies of the answers and counterclaims you drafted for Application Assignment 5 in your system folder, along with copies of or text page references to the sample answers, counterclaims, and cross-claims in this chapter.

10. From the steps for preparing and filing a third-party complaint, create a checklist for third-party practice and place it in your system folder. See Federal Forms 22A and 22B. Note any variations in local practice.

11. Make copies of the third-party summons, complaint, and motion and place them in your system folder, or make page references to these forms.

12. Enter page number references to or copies of the amended complaint and the notice of and motion to amend in your system folder.

13. Verify in the Pleadings, Motions, and Time Limits table the deadlines for amended pleadings set out in this chapter and in Rule 15. In addition, draft a checklist of procedures and time limits regarding amended pleadings and add it to the system folder.

14. Be sure to note the time requirements for a motion for judgment on the pleadings in the Pleadings, Motions, and Time Limits exhibit at the end of the chapter.

15. Place text page references to or copies of the motion, notice of motion, and affidavit in support of motion for summary judgment in your system folder.

16. Enter state time limits parallel to Rule 56 (summary judgment) in the Pleadings, Motions, and Time Limits exhibit at the end of the chapter. Fill in the state rule and deadline section up to the discovery section and add the table or page reference to your system folder.

17. Place a page reference to or a copy of the File Pleading Log in your system folder.

Application Assignments

1.   You are directed to look over a complaint for negligence. The body of the complaint reads as follows:

> 5.   On March 22, _____, Defendant owned and operated the Bay View Motel.

> 6.   On that date Plaintiff was descending a stairway at the motel, and as a result of Defendant's conduct, tripped and fell down the stairway.

7.   As a result of Defendant's conduct, Plaintiff suffered a broken wrist, a brain con-
cussion, and numerous bruises over much of his body.

8.   Because of the above injuries, Plaintiff had extensive medical bills and lost six
weeks of work, to the sum of $25,000.

Using the method suggested in the Determining What to Attack section, determine if
the body of this complaint is defective, and if so, why. Explain how the syllogism method of
finding defects applies to this case. Be prepared to defend your conclusion.

_____
_____
_____
_____

2.   Draft the Notice of Removal to have the case against Allen Howard removed to federal
court, as Mr. McDuff requested.

_____
_____
_____
_____

3.   Under Federal Rule 6(a) and (3) (where applicable), what are the following due dates?
   a.   Three days before a hearing on Monday, April 8.

_____
_____
_____
_____

   b.   Three months from February 16.

_____
_____
_____
_____

   c.   A complaint received on March 5 with an answer due in 20 days. On March 21, an
enlargement of time of 30 days is granted the defendant for filing the answer.

_____
_____
_____
_____

   d.   A complaint received on December 12.

_____
_____
_____
_____

   e.   When the original prescribed day to act is Friday but service was by electronic
means and the following Monday is not a legal holiday.

_____
_____
_____
_____

4.   Review the basic facts set out in Chapter 1 for Case IV, *Briar Patch Dolls, Inc. v. Teeny Tiny Manufacturing Co.*, a contract case. Using the method described in the Affirmative Defenses section of the text, make an initial determination of what affirmative defenses under the topic "discharge" might be available to the defendants. Make a list of these defenses and suggest some facts that might be necessary to support the defense. Because there are numerous defenses in contract law, confine yourself in this assignment to those defenses within the concept of "discharge."

_____
_____
_____
_____

5.   Exhibit 6:15 is a copy of the code (fact) complaint in Case II, Maple Meadows Campground case. Assume that your firm is defending the owner of the campground. Review the complaint and draft an Answer and Counterclaim for a code-pleading state. Then draft one for a notice-pleading jurisdiction.

_____
_____
_____
_____

Internet Exercises

1.   Using Westlaw, go to the directory (all databases) and locate the section on Litigation, then Forms, and then scroll to West's Federal Forms. Find the sample form titled Notice of Removal Based on Federal Law. What is the section number for this form? Using the form database, see if you can access forms for your state.

2.   Explore http://hotdocs.com to see what the service offers and what forms are available. What are some of this service's special features?

Additional Learning Exercises and Discussion Points

1.   What is the purpose of motions? What are the components of motions? What federal rules establish motion requirements?

_____
_____
_____

2.   What weaknesses in the complaint indicate a failure to state a claim and, thus, would be grounds for a motion to dismiss?

_____
_____
_____

3.   What grounds to dismiss a complaint are covered in Federal Rules of Civil Procedure 12(b)?

_____
_____
_____

4. Why should the motion to strike and the motion to make more definite and certain be kept in mind when you draft pleadings?

_____

_____

_____

5. What is the purpose of removal from state to federal court, and what strategic advantages may result?

_____

_____

_____

6. What defenses must be filed in motions previous to the answer or in the answer? Why is this important?

_____

_____

_____

7. What are the differences between denials and affirmative defenses?

_____

_____

_____

8. Research in a legal dictionary and write brief definitions for the defenses that must be alleged affirmatively under Federal Rule 8(c).

_____

_____

_____

9. Compare and contrast counterclaims and cross-claims.

_____

_____

_____

10. What may be changed or added in amendments to pleadings? What may not? Theorize about why this is so.

_____

_____

_____

11. What is the difference between a motion for judgment on the pleadings and motion for summary judgment?

_____

_____

_____

12. Work through the questions for study and review at the end of the chapter in the text to reinforce your understanding.

_____

_____

_____

Chapter Review Test and Answers

Review Test

Fill in the Blank

1. To accompany a motion, additional facts can be included in _____ _____ and legal authority in _____.

2. Where diversity exists between parties, removal to federal court is not permitted if the defendant is a citizen of the state where _____.

3. A special demurrer used in some states is similar to a _____ _____ when it is difficult to determine whether a claim has been stated.

4. Federal rules require the answer to be served within _____ days of receipt of summons or within _____ days after request for waiver was sent if defendant waived service of the summons.

5. A fact that defeats a claim, even though all the plaintiff's allegations are true is _____.

6. In third-party practice, if A is found liable then B owes A for the amount of the judgment, this is an example of _____; if A and B share the cost, this is _____.

True or False

T F 1.   Because electronic service of documents is fast, the time limit for responsive service is reduced by three days.

T F 2.   An acceptable way to gain time to prepare the answer is to file a motion to dismiss.

T F 3.   Parties generally cooperate in filing a joint application for an order for extension of time.

T F 4.   A response to a motion must be served not later than one day before the hearing on the motion.

T F 5.   Any type of case may be removed from state to federal court.

T F 6.   Argumentative denials are the most persuasive.

T F 7.   It is best not to plead inconsistent facts where verification is required.

T F 8.   Increasingly, an independent jurisdictional basis for a permissive counterclaim is not required for federal supplementary jurisdiction.

Multiple Choice

1. A motion must always be accompanied by
   a. an affidavit
   b. a notice of motion
   c. a memorandum of law
   d. all of the above

2. If a complaint is dismissed
   a. the lawsuit is over
   b. a demurrer must be filed
   c. the plaintiff will probably amend the complaint
   d. the defendant will probably amend the motion

3. A motion to strike seeks to rid a pleading of
   a. prejudicial language
   b. impertinent language
   c. insufficient defense
   d. all of the above

4. A response to a motion
   a. may be sufficient for a judge to deny the motion without a hearing
   b. can become the basis for a possible oral argument before the judge
   c. is unnecessary if there is a hearing
   d. may not include legal authority

5. Removal of an action from state to federal court
   a. may be requested by plaintiff
   b. is allowed only when state and federal jurisdictions are concurrent
   c. allows the advantage of a six-person jury
   d. is a constitutional right

6. Removal of an action from state court is permitted
   a. if unrelated to a federal question case
   b. in workers compensation cases
   c. by U.S. agencies and officers
   d. in all class action cases

7. Notice of removal should
   a. be served with the answer
   b. state facts in support of state jurisdiction
   c. state that all defendants have joined in the removal action
   d. remand the action to state court

8. Allegations in the complaint will be deemed admitted unless
   a. they are denied in the answer
   b. defendant files a motion to strike
   c. they do not state a cause of action
   d. they are part of a syllogism

9. Affirmative defenses are
   a. the same as denials
   b. available for only a few types of cases
   c. defined by substantive law
   d. defined by procedural law

10. Defenses to be alleged affirmatively include
    a. res gestae
    b. failure of payment
    c. latches and hinges
    d. estoppel

11. Pleadings may be amended in all the following except:
    a. within 20 days of service
    b. with leave of the court
    c. with written consent of opponent
    d. only before trial

12. A motion for summary judgment
    a. must allege that there is no question of fact
    b. must allege that there is no question of law
    c. must not include evidence
    d. must be filed before the answer

Short Answer

1. What are the basic requirements of a motion in Rule 7(b)?

_____
_____
_____

2. How can the syllogism method help you attack a complaint for the defendant?

_____
_____
_____

3. List four grounds for dismissing a complaint.

_____
_____
_____

4. What does an attorney's signature on a document mean?

_____
_____
_____

5. Give three strategic advantages for removing an action from state to federal court.

_____
_____
_____

6. According to Federal Rule 6(a), if a complaint is received on Friday, June 14, what is the last date for filing the answer within a 20-day time limit? What if the answer is electronically served?

_____
_____
_____

7. List four possible components of the answer.

_____
_____
_____

8. What is the penalty for claiming insufficient information to form a belief in the answer simply to avoid the work of investigation?

_____
_____
_____

9. How may a plaintiff respond to affirmative defenses?

_____

_____

_____

10. What is the difference between compulsory and permissive counterclaims?

_____

_____

_____

11. What is the purpose of impleader and what federal rule governs it?

_____

_____

_____

12. How can a file pleading log be important?

_____

_____

_____

Answers to Review Test

Fill in the Blank

1. an affidavit, a memorandum of law
2. the action is brought
3. motion to make more definite and certain
4. 20, 60
5. an affirmative defense
6. indemnification, joint liability

True or False	*Multiple Choice*	
1. F	1. b	8. a
2. F	2. c	9. c
3. T	3. d	10. d
4. T	4. b	11. d
5. F	5. b	12. a
6. F	6. c	
7. T	7. c	
8. T		

Short Answer

1. It must be in writing, except at trial or hearing,
    grounds stated with particularity setting forth order,
    same caption as complaint (et al. allowed),
    addresses of parties not necessary,
    attorney's signature and address is necessary.

2. 1.   Check that all minor premises (elements of law), including lack of defenses, are stated.
    2.   Check that major premise (law itself) is not misrepresented.

3. Lack of jurisdiction
    Improper venue
    Insufficiency of process
    Insufficiency of service of process
    Failure to state a claim

4. That attorney has read it,
    that it has or is likely to have evidentiary support,
    that it is warranted by law or good faith argument to alter law,
    that it is not offered for improper purposes,
    that any denials of federal contentions are warranted or reasonably based on lack of information or belief.

5. Different judge, more competent jury, a potentially less crowded docket, more liberal transfer rules, more complete discovery rules.

6. Friday, July 5, because it cannot be filed on July 4, a holiday. If e-service, July 8, because must add three days to July 5.

7. Legal defenses, admissions, denials, affirmative defenses, counterclaims, cross-claims.

8. A finding that the allegation is admitted or other Rule 11 sanctions.

9. Response is not required, but motion to strike or dismiss is allowed, or demurrer in some jurisdictions.

10. Compulsory counterclaims arise from original circumstances of the action and may not be the basis for a separate lawsuit. Permissive counterclaims may include unrelated claims, join other parties, and be the basis for a separate lawsuit.

11. Rule 14; to litigate at one time all claims that arise from a single set of circumstances.

12. It can help you keep track of the many time limits involved in filing pleadings.

 For additional resources, visit our Web site at **http://www.paralegal .delmar.cengage.com.**

Chapter 7. DISCOVERY AND ELECTRONIC DISCOVERY: OVERVIEW AND INTERROGATORIES

Chapter Objective

This chapter gives the student background information on disclosure and discovery, with considerable emphasis on the disclosure and discovery of e-information, its preservation, and the heightened relevance of pertinent ethics standards. Interrogatories, including those relevant to e-information, are presented in detail, helping you develop the knowledge, skills, and techniques needed to perform the tasks required of the paralegal when working in this area of discovery.

Outline

   E. Drafting Interrogatories
      1. Review Rules and Examples
      2. Introductory Paragraphs
      3. Definitions and Abbreviations
      4. Instructions
      5. Questions: The Body of Interrogatories
         a. General Background
         b. Pleadings
         c. Basic Areas of the Case
         d. Opinions and Legal and Factual Contentions
         e. Electronically Stored Information
         f. Concluding or Summary Interrogatories
   F. Drafting Techniques
   G. Concluding Material, Final Preparation, and Service of Interrogatories

III. Answering Interrogatories
   A. Note Deadline, Review Case File
   B. Review Possible Objections
   C. Review Questions
   D. Gather and Record Information
   E. Review Techniques for Answering Interrogatories
   F. Draft Answers and Have Them Reviewed, Signed, and Served
   G. Update Answers

IV. Analyzing the Answer and Compelling a Response

 V. Summary

Define

Discovery

_____

_____

Interrogatories

_____

_____

Workbook Assignments and Exercises

System Folder Assignments

1. In both the ethics and discovery sections of your system folder, place your own restatement of the ethical principles covered in this chapter, and cite the pertinent ethical rules.

2. Place page references or copies of the following items in their respective sections of your system folder. Add any suggestions from your instructor. Enter citations to the pertinent federal rules and your state rules on disclosure.
   • Preservation Letter
   • Form for Reporting Parties' Planning Meeting
   • Paralegal's Disclosure Checklist
   • Sample Interrogatories in E-Discovery Cases
   • Sample Interrogatories to Defendant (Auto Accident)

3.   Verify the deadlines for interrogatory practice by checking the Pleadings, Motions, and Time Limits table in Chapter 6 or in your system folder. Add the time limits from your state rules. Place citations to the pertinent federal and state rules in your system folder, including the number of interrogatories permitted by both federal and your state rules.

4.   Place a page reference to or a copy of the Checklist for Planning and Drafting Interrogatories, Exhibit 7:5, in your system folder. Supplement the checklist with any suggestions from your instructor.

5.   Create a form letter to the client from the letter in Exhibit 7:6 and place it in your system folder.

6.   Drawing from the interrogatory section of the chapter and any information added in class, draft a checklist for answering interrogatories and place it in your system folder. The checklist should cover the basic steps and techniques for preparing, drafting, serving, and updating interrogatories.

Application Assignments

1.   Drawing from the discussion on the scope and limitation of disclosure and discovery plus the pertinent rules of evidence discussed in Chapter 3, indicate whether the following would be discoverable in the *Ann Forrester* case. If an item would be discoverable only on a showing of undue hardship, indicate that as well. The first item is completed for you as an example. D = discoverable, ND = not discoverable, R = reason not discoverable, E = exceptional circumstances, H = undue hardship.

ANSWER:

ITEM	D	ND	R	E
1. Photo of accident scene taken by plaintiff's attorney		X	work product	H
2. Defendant Hart's driving schedule for day of accident and previous week				
3. Mercury Parcel's maintenance schedules on van				
4. Hart's statement to his attorney				
5. Forrester's medical bills				
6. Identification and opinion of plaintiff's trial expert on auto defects				
7. Statement Hart made to Mr. Forrester in plaintiff's possession				
8. Defense attorney's diagram of accident (not for trial exhibit)				
9. Forrester's alleged confession to her priest that she felt responsible for accident				
10. Plaintiff's request for a second copy of Hart's driving schedule				
11. Statement of Forrester tape recorded by her attorney's paralegal				
12. Letters between attorneys for defendants discussing strategy				

2.   Assume that a complaint was filed and served on the defendant in the *Forrester* case on Friday, March 29, or on another date supplied by your instructor. Using the Disclosure Time Frame Summary (Federal), determine the last possible date for the following:

    a.   The court scheduling conference

    b.   Parties' planning meeting

    c.   Report to court on parties' planning meeting

    d.   Disclosure from party joined on Tuesday, August 6

    e.   Objections to disclosure

    f.   Objections to any pretrial disclosure, assuming the trial date has been set for Monday, December 9

_____

_____

_____

_____

3.   Drawing from the material in this chapter on planning and drafting interrogatories (including the checklist in Exhibit 7:5) and using the form interrogatories as a guide, draft a set of carefully planned interrogatories on behalf of Ms. Forrester to Mercury Parcel Service. For the purposes of this assignment, confine your drafting to the following:

    a.   Caption and instructions

    b.   Questions on:

        1.   Background information, employment, and agency of Hart

        2.   Inadequate maintenance of van and possible defects

        3.   Time standards for operation of vehicles by drivers, and Hart and Mercury Parcel's compliance prior to accident

    c.   Concluding questions and directions

    d.   Signature and certificate of service

_____

_____

_____

_____

4.   To gain additional practice and confidence, reverse the situation and draft a set of interrogatories from Mercury Parcel to Ms. Forrester. Confine your drafting to:

    a.   Caption and instructions

    b.   Questions on:

        1.   Her background information (current employment information only)

        2.   Her statements to others about the accident

        3.   Her own possible negligence

    c.   Concluding questions and directions

    d.   Signature and certificate of service

_____

_____

_____

_____

5.   Exchange the interrogatories you drafted in assignments 3 and 4 with a classmate, then draft answers to the classmate's interrogatories, using the checklist you developed. For practice, object to at least one question and explain the basis of the objection. Also assume you do not trust the accuracy of the information you have for the answer to one other question. You may have to create some information to answer the questions adequately.

Or, assume that you are the paralegal whose firm is representing Carl Ameche in Case II, the campground fire case. Draft answers to several of the questions in the sample set of interrogatories (Exhibit 7:4). Also practice objections and how to respond when unsure of your information in your answers.

Or, answer your own interrogatories for practice and to evaluate the quality of your interrogatories. Use the requirements set out in the preceding paragraphs.

Internet Exercises

Find the ABA Civil Discovery Standards at the ABA site listed in Helpful Web Sites, then answer the following:

1. What standard or section deals with interrogatories?

2. According to the standard, when has a party fulfilled the obligation to respond to interrogatories?

3. What section covers technology?

4. Attorneys requesting the discovery of e-information should specify the preferred format in which the data should be produced. What are the two formats suggested and what is the subsection number?

Additional Learning Exercises and Discussion Points

1. List and define the seven major discovery devices.

2. What are two major limits to the scope of discovery?

3. Go to the law library and find at least five federal or state court decisions that found specific kinds of discovery requests not discoverable. List these and return to class ready to report the cases and the types of requests that were denied by the court.

4. When does a party have a duty to update discovery information? What is the applicable federal and state rules?

5.   Assume that you are a paralegal for a firm representing Make Tracks, Inc., Case III. In the discovery stage, your attorney asks you to draft as many questions as you can because she wants to "paper the plaintiff to death." She also says answer plaintiff's questions as narrowly as possible, and respond that requested safety test reports have been temporarily misplaced, even though you saw them in the file yesterday. What specific ethical concerns arise and what rules of professional conduct apply?

_____

_____

_____

6.   Work through the questions for study and review at the end of the chapter in the text to reinforce your understanding.

_____

_____

_____

Chapter Review Test and Answers

Review Test

Fill in the Blank

1. Pretrial disclosures include identification of a. _____,
   b. _____ and c. _____.

2. The list of things to address at the _____ meeting includes issues concerning the preservation of e-stored information.

3. A lawyer's legal opinion and tactical plans, called _____ _____ is protected from discovery.

4. The unintended revelation of privileged and protected information is the danger in choosing the Rule 33(d) option to have the requesting party examine the client's _____.

5. Unless otherwise authorized, discovery may not start until after _____ _____.

6. In answering interrogatories restating the question is called _____.

True or False

T F 1. Justice is better served when a case is tried on its merits than on surprise tactics.

T F 2. Discovery can lead to an early settlement.

T F 3. Mandatory disclosure replaces document production in discovery.

T F 4. The primary purpose of the preservation letter is to facilitate the return of privileged information.

T F 5. Under Federal Rule 26(f), attorneys must meet to plan disclosure and discovery.

T F 6. Insurance agreements likely to cover damages are revealed through discovery.

T F 7. Confidential information from the client must be revealed if it is requested through discovery.

T F 8. Discovery of computerized information requires no more than basic word processing skills.

T F 9. Updating discovery information is not necessary unless it is requested by the other side.

T F 10. A U.S. Supreme Court decision has facilitated discovery in international cases.

T F 11. Information requested in interrogatories must be admissible.

T F 12. Not all courts require that interrogatories be filed.

Multiple Choice

1. Mandatory disclosure does not include
   a. initial disclosure
   b. disclosure of information on expert testimony
   c. pretrial disclosure
   d. disclosure of trial preparation materials

2. Disclosure of information on expert testimony
   a. includes a statement of opinions
   b. is directed by the court or by stipulation between parties
   c. reveals the amount of compensation for the testimony
   d. all of the above
   e. a and c

3. Information is discoverable unless
   a. it is relevant
   b. it will lead to admissible evidence
   c. it is privileged
   d. all of the above

4. Alerting the opposing party to how easily e-information can be destroyed and facilitating the early prevention of loss of e-information is the aim of
   a. mandatory disclosure
   b. interrogatory practice
   c. the preservation letter
   d. the client communication ethics standard 1.4

5. Federal Rule 26(b)(5) requires a party withholding privileged information to
   a. provide identification of that information to the opposing party
   b. be penalized
   c. file an affidavit with the court
   d. reveal the information 30 days before trial

6. The federal court may limit the volume of discovery devices if
   a. the discovery requested is annoying to the opponent
   b. discovery requested is too expensive for the opponent's resources
   c. the information requested is privileged
   d. the parties are late in responding

7. In e-discovery, a refusal to produce requested e-information is most likely to apply to
   a. inexpensive production
   b. backup tapes and fragmented data
   c. business records
   d. current e-mails

8. Federal Rule 33 covers
   a. disclosure
   b. privileged communication
   c. paralegal ethics in discovery
   d. interrogatories

9. With mandatory disclosure, interrogatories
   a. are not allowed in federal court
   b. are limited to 25
   c. serve as a follow-up
   d. make depositions unnecessary
   e. b and c
   f. c and d

10. Interrogatories incorporate all the following components except:
    a. wherefore clause
    b. definitions and abbreviations
    c. summary interrogatories
    d. introductory paragraphs

11. Valid objections to interrogatories include
    a. information sought is a factual conclusion
    b. information sought is already known by opponent
    c. question seeks admission
    d. question is too broad

12. In answering interrogatories always
    a. save time by allowing the other party to search your client's records
    b. object in general to general questions
    c. avoid distortion or misrepresentation
    d. leave blank any questions you are unsure of

13. Interrogatories should be answered
    a. orally, if stipulated by all parties
    b. under oath
    c. without objection
    d. without revealing the true answer
    e. all of the above

14. If the answer to an interrogatory is unavailable or uncertain, you should
    a. leave a blank
    b. indicate supplements will follow
    c. state on information or belief
    d. state based on secondhand information
    e. all but a
    f. all but d

Short Answer

1. List the seven discovery devices from Federal Rule 26.

   _____
   _____
   _____

2. Once the recipient party is notified that the opponent has produced privileged information, what are the recipient party's options under Rule 26(b)(5)?

   _____
   _____
   _____

3. What are the advantages of interrogatories?

   _____
   _____
   _____

4. How can your understanding of the elements of the case help you in drafting interrogatories?

   _____
   _____
   _____

5. You need to find out if the defendant's automobile had defects in the steering column, brakes, exhaust, or electrical circuits during the year of the accident and also during the preceding year. Write one simple interrogatory question to elicit these multiple answers.

_____

_____

_____

6. Why is it important to word interrogatories carefully?

_____

_____

_____

7. When interrogatory answers are returned needing clarification, what are the options?

_____

_____

_____

8. Why is it a good idea to copy interrogatories submitted to you?

_____

_____

_____

Answers to Review Test

Fill in the Blank

1. a. witness who may be called at trial,
   b. witnesses who will testify by deposition, and
   c. documents and exhibits
2. parties' planning
3. trial preparation materials or attorney work product
4. business records
5. the parties' planning meeting
6. engrossing

True or False

1. T	7. F
2. T	8. F
3. F	9. F
4. F	10. T
5. T	11. F
6. T	12. T

Multiple Choice

1. d	8. d
2. d	9. e
3. c	10. a
4. c	11. d
5. a	12. c
6. b	13. b
7. b	14. e

Short Answer

1. disclosure, interrogatories, depositions, production and inspection, expert opinion, medical exams, request for admissions

2. To return promptly, sequester, or destroy the information; must not disclose it; must seek to recover information if already disclosed or challenge the claim of protection while preserving the challenged information.

3. They are relatively inexpensive, the answering party has a duty to find the answer, can "pierce the corporate veil."

4. Questions need to elicit evidence to support those elements.

5. Please identify all defects in the automobile from 20___ to 20___.

6. You save time by eliciting the wanted information the first time and without causing objections.

7. The attorney takes over.
   You request more information from opposing representation.
   You draft, file, and serve a motion to compel and affidavit.

8. You can enter notes on working copy; facilitates analysis of interrogatories and preparation of answers.

 For additional resources, visit our Web site at **http://www.paralegal .delmar.cengage.com.**

Chapter 8. DISCOVERY: DEPOSITIONS

Chapter Objective

Chapter 8 continues the study of discovery with a focus on depositions. After an introduction to the topic, you learn specific tasks required of paralegals in deposition practice. The final section offers background and techniques for digesting depositions and other documents.

Outline

I. Depositions
    A. Introduction
    B. Scope and Limits of the Deposition
    C. Types of Depositions
    D. Procedure
    E. Preliminary Tasks
        1. Determine Whom to Depose
            a. Organize Information to Identify Potential Deponents
            b. Designated Corporate or Agency Deponent
            c. Expert Witnesses
        2. Conduct a Preliminary Interview
    F. Coordinate the Deposition
        1. Arrange for Site and Necessary Components
            a. Time
            b. Site
            c. Method of Recording
            d. Oath Officer
            e. Deposition Tracking Logs
        2. Prepare and Serve Notice of the Deposition
        3. Subpoena the Deponent
            a. Obtain the Subpoena
            b. HIPAA and Subpoenas
            c. Attach Fees
            d. Serve the Subpoena
    G. Prepare for Deposition
        1. Draft Questions or an Examination Outline
        2. Gather and Prepare Documents and Exhibits
        3. Set Up Witness Files
        4. Assist in the Preparation of the Client or Witness for Testimony
    H. Attend and Review the Deposition

II. Digesting Depositions and Other Documents
    A. Introduction and Definition
    B. Purposes for Digesting Depositions
    C. Techniques for Digesting Depositions
    D. Types of Deposition Digests and Indexes
    E. Digest Aids for Complex Cases
    F. Automated Deposition Summaries
    G. Other Follow-Up Tasks

III. Summary

Define

Deposition

_____
_____

Deponent

_____
_____

Subpoena

_____
_____

Subpoena duces tecum

_____
_____

Workbook Assignments and Exercises

System Folder Assignments

1.   Write a brief outline on the definition, purpose, scope, and the procedure of depositions to place in your system folder.

2.   Add or verify the deadlines for deposition practice from your state and local federal district rules in the Pleadings, Motions, and Time Limits exhibit in Chapter 6 or in your system folder. Place citations to the pertinent state or federal rules, including those covering scope and other limitations on depositions, in your system folder.

3.   Draft a checklist on preparing and serving subpoenas and place it and references to the pertinent documents in your system folder. Include citations to both state and federal rules. Note the time limits for objection to a subpoena in this section of your system folder and in your Pleadings, Motions, and Time Limits exhibit. Add a section to the checklist on the relationship between a subpoena duces tecum and HIPAA procedural requirements. Place a copy or the page reference to the HIPAA compliant Sample Cover Letter to Records Custodian in your system folder.

4.   Draft a checklist for planning and preparing for deposition based on the steps and recommendations made in this chapter, and place it in your system folder.

5.   Place a copy of or a page reference to the Checklist for Preparing Witness Files in your system folder.

6.   Place a copy of or a page reference to the Letter to Client Regarding Deposition in your system folder.

7.   Prepare a checklist for attending and reviewing the deposition and place it in your system folder.

8.   Place copies of or page references to the deposition summary examples in this chapter in your system folder. Add any other examples provided in class.

Application Assignments

1.   Assume you represent Mr. Hart. Prepare a deposition outline for your attorney to use in examining Ms. Forrester. For purposes of this assignment only, limit the scope of your outline to the time immediately before and during the accident. Do not get into injuries or other damages. Try using a tape recorder if one is available to dictate questions or topics. Use the sample outline, your checklist, and Exhibits 8:4 and 8:5 as guides for your work.

_____
_____
_____
_____

2.   Exhibit 8:10 contains excerpts from a deposition of Mr. Hart. Skim the deposition transcript first. Then read it and carefully draft the corresponding section of a chronological digest. Prepare a table of contents for the digest. Count lines from the top of each page of the deposition, since no lines are provided. Then do a topical summary. Use a computer and appropriate software to do the summaries.

_____
_____
_____
_____

Internet Exercises

1.   Go to the _Concordance_ and _Summation_ Web sites. Compare the features and costs of each service. Try a demonstration of the product, if possible. Which product would you recommend and why?

2.   Using the Deponet service, locate a legal videographer and a court reporter in your area.

3.   Go to one of the three online, real-time deposition transcript services and survey its features and costs.

Additional Learning Exercises and Discussion Points

1.   What limits are imposed on what can be asked in a deposition? What federal and state rules apply?

_____
_____
_____

2.   How do you gather a list of persons who might be deposed? How can you narrow that list?

_____
_____
_____

3. What are some of the ways to take depositions, other than orally, and their governing rules? What are the advantages and disadvantages of such procedures?

ANSWER:

Method	Advantage	Disadvantage	Rule

4. Assume that Herbert Herbert, III, is the executive officer for Mercury Parcel Service, Inc. Draft a subpoena duces tecum requiring Mr. Herbert to appear at a deposition and to bring the employment and safety records of Mr. Hart. Find information in the Forrester complaint in Chapter 4 and make up remaining information, remembering the rules for deposing persons in another district.

5. Why is it important to prepare a client or witness for a deposition? In what ways can a paralegal assist at such a preparation conference?

6. Assume that you are working to prepare Mr. Hart for his deposition by Ms. Forrester's attorney. Mr. Hart says that he is unsure about the road conditions at the time of the accident. You and the attorney know that it works against Hart to appear unsure about important facts.

   a. The attorney says to Hart, "It's best not to be unsure and, after all, the road was not very icy." Are there any ethical concerns?

   b. The attorney has left the room and you say, "Mr. Hart, do you recall that during our first interview you told me the road was not very icy?" Are there any ethical concerns?

7. In what ways can a computer assist you in summarizing a deposition?

_____

_____

_____

8. Describe a narrative deposition digest and state its advantages.

_____

_____

_____

9. Review the text section on digesting the deposition. Create a list of techniques for digesting a deposition.

_____

_____

_____

10. Work through the questions for study and review at the end of the chapter in the text to reinforce your understanding.

_____

_____

_____

Chapter Review Test and Answers

Review Test

Fill in the Blank

1. In jurisdictions where judges do not sign subpoenas, HIPAA and the
_____ require written assurance that the pertinent patient has been
notified of the intent to subpoena the records.

True or False

T F 1.   Depositions are used to evaluate the opposing attorney.

T F 2.   If a witness dies before trial, that witness's deposition may not be used.

T F 3.   Since depositions are expensive, they are rarely used.

T F 4.   Normally, no more than 10 depositions are allowed.

T F 5.   A deposition by written questions is best because the other party cannot ask cross
questions.

T F 6.   The party requesting the deposition must pay recording costs.

T F 7.   When a deposition may be taken depends only on the deponent.

T F 8.   Generally deponents may not be required to travel long distances to the deposition
site.

T F 9.   In the federal system, an attorney can issue a subpoena for a deposition.

T F 10. Subpoenas in the federal system are served by a marshal.

T F 11. An objection to a subpoena can be served any time before the deposition.

T F 12. It is a good idea to interview the witness before a deposition is planned.

T F 13. Good objections suggest answers to the deponent.

T F 14. An Arrangements Checklist is one type of deposition tracking log.

Multiple Choice

1. Advantages of depositions include
   a. only parties may be questioned
   b. deponents may be deposed for a full 10 hours
   c. answers can be used at trial
   d. no notice to parties is needed

2. A deposition may be taken without leave of court under Rule 26(a) only if
   a. the deponent is not a party
   b. the deponent does not have an attorney
   c. the deposition takes place outside the jurisdiction of the court
   d. the parties' planning meeting has taken place.

3. A videotape of the deposition is advantageous because
   a. a good quality tape is easy to produce
   b. a laboratory demonstration can be shown
   c. editing can make the testimony more effective
   d. it makes summarizing the deposition easier

4. A deposition cannot be used against a party
   a. for impeachment
   b. who received less than 11 days notice
   c. who after due diligence obtains counsel
   d. who does not appear with records subject to a subpoena duces tecum

5. A party to be deposed must receive a
   a. subpoena
   b. court order
   c. notice of deposition
   d. summons

6. The document needed for commanding a person to bring documents to a deposition is
   a. subpoena duces tecum
   b. subpoena
   c. summons
   d. quasi in rem

7. A subpoena is issued by a clerk in the federal system in
   a. the district where the deposition is to be taken
   b. any district that has jurisdiction
   c. the location most convenient for the deponent
   d. the district where the action is pending

8. Subpoenas are usually issued
   a. in medias res
   b. in toto
   c. in forma pauperis
   d. in blank

9. Documents or photos may be introduced at depositions so that
   a. the deponent can be convinced of your client's position
   b. they can be authenticated
   c. they can be verified
   d. all of the above

10. When preparing witnesses for testimony
    a. they should review all recorded statements
    b. tell them the answers they should give
    c. tell them to be impartial
    d. tell them to answer questions quickly

11. If the deponent refuses to sign the deposition transcript, it is signed by
    a. the court reporter
    b. the judge
    c. the attorneys
    d. no one

12. Inconsistencies in deposition testimony
    a. are sufficient reason for a second deposition
    b. make the deposition useless
    c. are irrelevant
    d. can be used to impeach a witness

13. Changes to the deposition transcript can be made by
    a. the attorney
    b. the deponent
    c. the court reporter
    d. no one

14. Deposition digests are used to
    a. index testimony
    b. reveal inconsistencies in testimony
    c. record complete language of transcripts
    d. review for trial
    e. all but a
    f. all but c

15. Stating the method of recording is required for
    a. the Items Sent to Witness log
    b. a topical deposition summary
    c. HIPAA compliance
    d. a subpoena for a deposition

Short Answer

1. Three types of depositions are:

   _____

   _____

   _____

   _____

2. Compare the scope of questioning at a deposition to that at trial.

   _____

   _____

   _____

   _____

3. Why is preparation of your client for a deposition important?

   _____

   _____

   _____

4. What is the paralegal's role at deposition?

   _____

   _____

   _____

5. List three types of deposition digests.

   _____

   _____

   _____

Answers to Review Test

Fill in the Blank

1. health care provider

True or False				*Multiple Choice*			
1. T		7. F		1. d		8. d	
2. F		8. T		2. d		9. b	
3. F		9. T		3. b		10. c	
4. T		10. F		4. b		11. a	
5. F		11. F		5. c		12. d	
6. T		12. T		6. a		13. b	
		13. F		7. a		14. f	
		14. T				15. d	

Short Answer

1. Oral exam, written question, before action is filed.

2. Deposition allows more latitude—questions that might reasonably lead to evidence: hearsay, identification of witnesses and evidence.

3. Effective testimony may bring the case to an early and favorable settlement. Inconsistencies in the deposition will damage your client's case.

4. Listen; take notes on information, objections, effectiveness of witness, and opposing counsel; catch missed questions; retrieve information and documents.

5. chronological (sequential or page/line), topical (category, subject), narrative.

 For additional resources, visit our Web site at **http://www.paralegal .delmar.cengage.com.**

Chapter 9. DISCOVERY: DOCUMENT PRODUCTION AND CONTROL, MEDICAL EXAMS, ADMISSIONS, AND COMPELLING DISCOVERY

Chapter Objective

The purpose of this chapter is to provide you with techniques and practice in further discovery procedures: document production (including e-information, spoliation, and preservation), medical examinations, and admissions, as well as the informal use of the Freedom of Information Act. You also learn the procedure for compelling discovery. Along with each discovery device come guidelines for producing, reviewing, and organizing information.

Outline

Define

Redaction

_____

_____

_____

Automated litigation support

_____

_____

_____

Workbook Assignments and Exercises

System Folder Assignments

1.   In separate subsections of your system folder for production of documents and things and entry upon land for inspection and other things; request for physical and mental examination; request for admissions; and objections, compelling discovery, and sanctions, insert the following:

    Outline on definition, purpose, scope, applicable rules, and procedures;

    Text page references, a copy or your own draft of pertinent checklists, techniques, and tips;

    Copies of relevant sample forms for each device.

2.   Note parallel state rules and time limits for each of the above discovery devices in the Pleadings, Motions, and Time Limits Chart (Exhibit 6:25) and in each respective subsection of your system folder.

3.   Draft a procedural checklist for making a request pursuant to the Freedom of Information Act, both federal and state, and place it in your system folder. Include a copy of or page reference to the sample FOIA request in the chapter.

4.   In a subsection in your system folder on organizing files, insert text page references to or your drafted checklists for organizing small and large case files, copies of the master and subfile indexes, any alternative methods for organizing case files, and your organized case file to date for the *Forrester* case. (See relevant Application Assignment 5 below.)

Application Assignments

1.   Draft a response to Ms. Forrester's request for production of documents and things found in this chapter.

_____

_____

_____

_____

2.   Using the Mini-Guide in Appendix D, interpret the physician's orders for Mrs. Forrester's hospital treatment in Figure A:4, then compare your interpretation with the translation in Figure A:5.

_____

_____

_____

_____

3.   Using the procedures described in this chapter, the form in Exhibit 9:8, and examples of the types and forms of questions to ask, draft a five-item set of requests for admissions from Ms. Forrester to Mercury Parcel that covers:
- Caption
- Admissions on employment and agency of Hart
- Admissions on forms that reflect irregular maintenance—as well as inaction on complaint about wheels locking when braking

Draft requests for admissions regarding both documents and statements. Assume that you have previously discovered certain facts needed to justify the requests.

_____
_____
_____
_____

4.   Assume that you are a paralegal for Mercury Parcel and have received the following requests for admissions from Forrester's attorney:

    a.   Defendant Hart was an employee of Mercury Parcel Service, Inc. on Tuesday, February 23, ___.
    b.   Plaintiff Forrester's conduct did not negligently contribute to the accident on February 26, ___.
    c.   No follow-up maintenance was performed on vehicle 23 regarding locking wheels between the time of the filing of the complaint and the accident on February 26, ___ as confirmed by the unchecked follow-up item on form ICC-2015, No. 37.
    d.   Defendant Hart's supervisor John Roosevelt, was advised to tell Defendant Hart not to fill out a company accident report after the accident.

Reflect on each item and draft what you think would be the proper response to each item. Your responses should vary. Use the format that follows:
REQUEST NO. 1: Defendant Hart . . .
RESPONSE: (Admit, Deny, Other)

5.   Collect the documents you have gathered so far in the _Forrester_ case and organize a small case file.

_____
_____
_____
_____

Internet Exercises

1.   Go to the Department of Justice site on the motion to compel discovery. What databases is the plaintiff seeking?

2.   Search listed Helpful Web Sites, http://www.paralegals.org, or http://www.nala.org for articles on discovery techniques or document management and case management (litigation) software. Briefly summarize the main points of two articles.

Additional Learning Exercises and Discussion Points

1.   What are the purposes, objectives, and concerns for the production of documents?

_____
_____
_____

2.   To better understand and retain an overall picture of the document production process, draft a chronological list of the procedural steps in the federal production process. (See the Procedure subsection at the beginning of the chapter.)

_____
_____
_____

3.   You are asked to draft a request for the production of documents under Rule 34(a) of the Federal Rules of Civil Procedure. The request is to get pertinent documents from Mercury Parcel Service concerning safety and vehicle maintenance. You have no idea what forms are common to this industry. How might you determine what to ask for?

_____

_____

_____

4.   You work for the law firm representing Teeny Tiny Manufacturing (Case IV). Your attorney wants to see Briar Patch's documents indicating the number of pieces received and, particularly, the number of unsatisfactory pieces. Further, it is necessary to inspect a generous sampling of the unsatisfactory pieces to see if they were justifiably rejected. Draft the needed request for production.

_____

_____

_____

5.   For organizational purposes, how should documents be produced in the reply [34(b)(i)]? What limitations and protections apply to the form in which e-information must be produced?

_____

_____

_____

6.   Briefly explain the importance to a business client of a document retention policy.

_____

_____

_____

7.   Place a copy of or a page reference to the Initial Steps Checklist for Preparing for Production of Documents and Things in your system folder.

_____

_____

_____

8.   What advantages does the standardized decimal document numbering system provide over other systems?

_____

_____

_____

9.   What is the danger of requesting a copy of the report of the requested medical exam? What rule applies?

_____

_____

_____

10. What is the role of the paralegal at a Rule 35 medical exam?

_____

_____

_____

11. Interpret or define the following medical notes or terms using the Mini-Guide to Interpreting Medical Records in Appendix D of the text.
    a.   DIA: FX Mid 1/3 ® tibia

_____

_____

b.   VS q 3h; CBC, lytes; 2 u in am

_____

_____

_____

c.   NPO; TLC; T 98^6; P 82; R 18

_____

_____

_____

d. H_2O_2 qd

_____

_____

_____

e.   Anorexia:

_____

_____

_____

Gastrointeritis:

_____

_____

_____

Epilepsy:

_____

_____

_____

Encephalitis:

_____

_____

_____

12. Assume that you have been assigned to a very complex litigation case involving a series of construction contracts for a downtown mall, office, and residential center. You have never worked in this highly technical field. Explain in general terms how you would pre-pare a Mini-Guide to Construction Records to assist you in interpreting such records over the next three years of litigation.

_____

_____

_____

13. In Case V from Chapter 1, assume that Carlos Montez has refused Ms. Rakowski's request to produce reports of previous incidents of harassment. He has objected on the grounds that this is irrelevant. Briefly stating that this may lead to relevant evidence, draft a motion to compel the answer.

_____

_____

_____

14. What remedies are available for overreaching discovery requests? What are the applicable federal rule and state equivalent? Note these in your system folder.

_____
_____
_____

15. Using the small case filing method described in the text, under which of the four general categories and, if pertinent, in what order would you place the following:

  a.   a letter to Ms. Forrester dated December 2 of this year
  b.   the complaint
  c.   a motion to dismiss the complaint
  d.   a time slip carbon for 3 hours of legal research
  e.   the client's background sheet
  f.   a memorandum on the admissibility of inflammatory photographs
  g.   client's medical bills
  h.   a letter to Ms. Forrester dated May of this year
  i.   note on fee paid to witness for deposition
  j.   a memo from you to Isadora Pearlman
  k.   a written statement by Ms. Schnabel

  ANSWER:

  FACTS   PLEADINGS   CORRESPONDENCE   BILLINGS

16. When organizing and working with complex case files, one component is almost indispensable for organization and retrieval. What is this component?

_____
_____
_____

17. Work through the questions for study and review at the end of the chapter in the text to reinforce your understanding.

_____
_____
_____

Chapter Review Test and Answers

Review Test

Fill in the Blank

1. The normal response time within which to reply to a request for production of documents is _____ days.

2. Electronically stored information must be produced in the form in which it is ordinarily maintained or that is _____.

3. The final decision on document production methods is made by _____
_____.

4. When you take original files for production, it is wise to leave_____ or
_____ for the custodian.

5. Documenting the _____ of custody is essential to securing e-stored information.

6. At the close of the case, original documents should be_____ indices should be _____, and copies of documents should be _____.

7. Production of documents and things is particularly helpful in ————————————
_____ cases.

8. Adverse parties request _____ to prevent fraudulent claims of injury.

True or False

T F 1.   If the form in which to produce e-stored information is not indicated in the request to produce documents and things, the responding party must state the form in which it intends to produce the information.

T F 2.   The party requesting the production of documents and things usually pays for procedures that facilitate that party's own analysis of the documents.

T F 3.   Failure to organize documents can mean the loss of the case.

T F 4.   The original source log is especially helpful when files are pulled for production.

T F 5.   Produced documents belonging to the same category should be stapled together.

T F 6.   A great advantage of "imaging" documents is quick retrieval.

T F 7.   Federal Rule 37 covers requests for medical examinations.

T F 8.   Paralegals should not accompany clients to medical exams.

T F 9.   A request for a medical examination does not require the party to undergo the exam.

T F 10. If a party fails to cooperate in discovery, sanctions on that party could include default or dismissal of the action.

Multiple Choice

1. The purpose of document production is to
   a. skillfully confuse the opponent with a mass of paper
   b. provide the parties with an opportunity to review pertinent documents
   c. prevent opponent's access to documents
   d. provide the parties with unrestricted access to the opponent's documents

2. The preservation letter and the litigation hold aim to prevent
   a. spoliation
   b. document retention
   c. overreaching production requests
   d. abuse of the request for physical examination

3. Help in locating specific documents for production can come from
   a. the client
   b. the client's technology manager
   c. company division heads
   d. all of the above

4. Estimating costs and meeting with the client's key personnel are important
   a. procedures while screening pulled documents
   b. initial steps for requesting admissions
   c. initial steps for document production preparation
   d. procedures dictated by the federal rules on production of documents

5. The initial volume of data captured for production of e-stored information can be substantially reduced by
   a. imaging all paper documents
   b. obtaining mirror data images of opponent's computers
   c. including all replicant data
   d. using sophisticated data filtering programs

6. When you screen files and documents for production you should
   a. identify items responsive to the request
   b. identify privileged documents
   c. number and classify documents
   d. all of the above

7. Screening "pulled" documents involves
   a. paper documents only
   b. highlighting unresponsive items
   c. redacting relevant information
   d. numbering and coding

8. When copying documents for production
   a. staple copies if originals were stapled
   b. copy only the pertinent pages of large documents
   c. keep any poor copies for use as scratch paper
   d. take copies for the case file and return originals to the custodian

9. An adverse jury instruction can result from
   a. a breach of the duty of confidentiality
   b. the waiver of privileged information
   c. a breach of the duty to preserve evidence
   d. all of the above

10. A medical exam may be ordered only if
    a. the alleged condition is in controversy
    b. the party is a child
    c. all HIPAA requirements are met
    d. the party's privacy will not be violated

11. A party may request admissions on
    a. facts
    b. genuineness of evidence
    c. application of law to facts
    d. all of the above

12. A request for admission seeks to
    a. discover new evidence
    b. narrow the issues for trial
    c. confirm the admissibility of evidence
    d. all of the above

13. The fact section of a small case file should include
    a. the complaint
    b. medical bills
    c. records of witness fees
    d. letters from the client

14. The small case file does not need
    a. a numbering system
    b. an index
    c. chronological order
    d. subgroupings

15. Large case files usually
    a. have to be organized by different methods for each case
    b. are no more complex than small case files
    c. do not need indices if they are organized properly
    d. are divided and subdivided numerically

Short Answer

1. Identify the three major steps to protecting a client from sanctions for failure to preserve evidence.

_____
_____
_____

2. List the cost hierarchy of producing e-stored data from the least expensive to the most expensive.

_____
_____
_____

3. How does a uniform decimal system of numbering documents work?

_____
_____
_____

4. Describe the process for handling privileged documents in screening and preparing the documents for production.

_____
_____
_____

5. What entity of the ABA tests software for law offices and can provide assistance in choosing a program?

_____

_____

_____

6. Name three helpful resources for interpreting technical documents.

_____

_____

_____

7. How can a master topical digest help organize depositions?

_____

_____

_____

8. What are the advantages in using the Freedom of Information Act for discovery?

_____

_____

_____

9. What are four general categories to be included in a small case file?

_____

_____

_____

10. What indexes are necessary for a large case file?

_____

_____

_____

Answers to Review Test

Fill in the Blank

1. 30
2. reasonably usable
3. the attorney
4. a checkout card and/or replacement sheet
5. chain
6. returned to custodians, kept in case file, destroyed
7. business
8. medical exams

True or False			*Multiple Choice*					
1. T	7. F		1. b		7. d		13. b	
2. T	8. F		2. a		8. a		14. a	
3. T	9. T		3. d		9. b		15. d	
4. F	10. T		4. c		10. a			
5. F			5. d		11. d			
6. T			6. e		12. b			

Short Answer

1 Document retention policy, fully inform client of duty to preserve and consequences of spoliation, and promptly notify client when the potential for litigation is real.

2. Active, metadata, replicant, backup, and residual (fragmented).

3. Digits in each position of the number refer to a specific category to which the document belongs, allowing it to be organized and retrieved for a specific purpose.

4. Identify and log privileged documents, extract them from production set, and place them in a separate paper or electronic folder. If paper, pull the colored privileged document sheet and leave a substitute sheet with the document number. Redact the privileged portion of the document and return a redacted version to the production set with an explanation for the redaction. Prepare privilege log for opponent. Secure all privileged documents.

5. The Legal Technology Advisory Council

6. Medical records librarian, specialized dictionaries, textbooks, professional organizations, etc.

7. It brings together information from all depositions in a case on one topic.

8. Can be used without filing an action, relevance does not apply, access is available to anyone with bona fide request, not restricted to information from a party

9. Facts, pleadings, correspondence, billing

10. Master index, subfile indexes.

 For additional resources, visit our Web site at **http://www.paralegal .delmar.cengage.com.**

Chapter 10. SETTLEMENT AND OTHER ALTERNATIVE DISPUTE RESOLUTIONS

Chapter Objective

The purpose of this chapter is to familiarize you with the settlement process, applicable federal and state rules of civil procedure, formulas and processes for calculating damages, and forms common to settlement. Arbitration and mediation are presented.

Outline

I. Introduction

II. Settlement
    A. Introduction
        1. Definition and Purpose
        2. The Role of the Paralegal
        3. Ethical Consideration
    B. Preparing for Settlement
        1. Introduction
        2. Early Investigation and Collection of Information
            a. Introduction
            b. Party's Social or Business Background
            c. Party's Medical Condition
            d. Party's Commercial Condition
            e. Special Areas of Investigation
        3. Communicate with Client and Insurance Adjuster
        4. Calculating Damages
    C. Presenting the Settlement Request
        1. Introduction
        2. Settlement Precis or Letter
        3. Settlement Brochure (Demand Package)
        4. Video: "Day in the Life"
        5. Calendaring
    D. Role of the Defendant's or Insurance Company's Paralegal
    E. Preparing for the Pretrial Conference
    F. Settlement Conference

III. Settlement Forms
    A. Releases and Settlement Agreements
    B. Stipulation and Order for Dismissal
    C. Consent Decree and Order
    D. Settlement Distribution Statement

IV. Other Alternative Dispute Resolutions: Arbitration, Mediation, and Summary Trials
    A. Introduction
    B. Arbitration
    C. Mediation
    D. Early Case Assessment

Define

Settlement

_____

_____

Settlement precis

_____

_____

Release

_____

_____

Without prejudice

_____

_____

With prejudice

_____

_____

Adjudication on the merits

_____

_____

Arbitration

_____

_____

Mediation

_____

_____

Med-Arb

_____

_____

Summary trial

_____

_____

Workbook Assignments and Exercises

System Folder Assignments

1.   In the ethics section of your system folder, add page references to ethical considerations for the settlement process, the cited sections of the Model Rules of Professional Conduct, and the rules or ethical standards in your state.

2.   Draft a checklist of or enter text page references to the items that need to be researched and summarized in preparation for settlement. Indicate the sources for such information. Place the checklist in the settlement section of your system folder.

3.   Place a copy of or page reference to the Damage Summary and Worksheet (Exhibit 10:1) in your system folder.

4.   Place a page reference or copies of the Pretrial Conference Preparation Checklist and the attorney's authorization from the client to settle in your system folder.

5.   Add page references or copies of each of the settlement forms and the outline of the pretrial memorandum to your system folder. If time permits, draft each form at least once and adapt it to the *Forrester* case.

Application Assignments

1.   What factors either favoring or discouraging settlement do you see present in the *Forrester* case? Discuss.

_____
_____
_____
_____

2.   Why would any of the matters characterized at the end of the Party's Medical Condition section as the "three strikes" work against the plaintiff? How might you overcome each of the strikes?

_____
_____
_____
_____

3.   Using your imagination to provide missing facts, draft a settlement precis or settlement letter for the *Forrester* case. Critique these in small groups with your fellow students. Place the settlement precis or letter in your system folder. Keep in mind that a well-drafted *Forrester* precis or settlement letter as part of a well-drafted system folder can be impressive when offered as a writing sample to a future employer.

_____
_____
_____
_____

4.   Draft an outline of the contents of a settlement brochure for the *Forrester* case indicating what should appear and in what order. Compare your list of components and discuss the advantages of each in small groups with class members. Make a list of the typical components of a settlement brochure and place it in your system folder.

   In the alternative, individual class members can accept responsibility for roughly equal parts of a *Forrester* settlement brochure. When finished, the students assigned to one part can meet, compare their individual work, and compile a model section. Eventually the various model sections can be photocopied and shared to arrive at the best complete brochure.

_____
_____
_____
_____

5.   By researching your state statutes and local federal rules, determine whether your state has a provision for arbitration or mediation. If so, determine what types of cases and dispute amounts are considered for the program. If your state has no such system, write a proposal to your local newspaper on why you believe there should or shouldn't be such a system. Discuss and defend your proposals in class.

_____
_____
_____
_____

Internet Exercises

1.   Go to MoreLaw.com. What is the current highest damage award of the month? Was it achieved through settlement or trial?

2.   Go to JuryVerdicts.com. What is the jury verdict publisher for your state or the nearest state where a publisher is available? What information does the publisher offer?

3.   In the American Arbitration Association site, find the ADR revised code of ethics. What are the subjects of five substantive changes listed for the 2004 revised code?

Additional Learning Exercises and Discussion Points

1.   Assume that the Congletons, the campground owners in Case II, are told by you that their attorney, your supervisor, advises them to agree to settle their case by paying Mr. Ameche $60,000. The Congletons say no and want to go to trial. Your attorney believes that the jury will hold the Congletons liable for $150,000.

      a.   Considering that lawyers are supposed to exercise their independent judgment, may the attorney ethically accept the offer since it is such a good one?

_____
_____
_____

      b.   Are there any other ethical concerns raised in this scenario?

_____
_____
_____

2.   What is the importance of gearing timetables and preparation to the settlement process? The advantages?

_____
_____
_____

3.   What are LOELs and why would a plaintiff want these separated from damages for pain and suffering? Do you think people ought to receive such damages? What is the problem with such damages?

_____
_____
_____

4.   Which of the following are special damages and which are general?
   a. hospital bill   d. horror of injury   g. pain
   b. wages lost   e. loss of stimulation of job   h. loss of status
   c. LOELs   f. lost household services

   Special damages:
   General damages:

5.   Calculate the damage amounts in the following fact situation (show calculations on workbook page): Darlene Rakowski's damages based on $500 of embarrassment per day for 100 days, $250 of anxiety per day over losing job for 20 days, lost wages for days caused to miss work at $85 per day for 20 days, psychiatric counselling at $100 per session, 1 session per week for 8 weeks. Future psychiatric sessions, 10 per year for next 5 years with reduction to present cash value of 5 percent. Assume medical costs will go up 8 percent per year.

_____
_____
_____

6.   What should be included in the cover letter that goes to the opponent with the settlement brochure?

_____
_____
_____

7.   If you work for the defendant, and the plaintiff sends summarized medical reports and witness statements rather than originals, what should you do?

_____
_____
_____

8.   Describe the purposes of Rule 16 of the Federal Rules of Civil Procedure. Does your state rule on settlement contain these broad purposes?

_____
_____
_____

9.   What is a pretrial statement (memorandum) and what is one of its advantages?

_____
_____
_____

10. Research to determine if your state requires consideration to validate a release and to see if a covenant not to sue is required.

_____
_____
_____

11. Using the Settlement Agreement form provided in Exhibit 10:8 of the text or your state's form and information on the *Forrester* case or other case as assigned by your instructor, draft a settlement agreement that reflects a fair settlement in the case.

_____
_____
_____

12. What are the primary reasons for the use of alternative dispute resolution?

_____

_____

_____

13. After reading the Bruno Arbitration case, what are your impressions about the outcome of this case?

_____

_____

_____

14. Assume that Teeny Tiny Manufacturing and Briar Patch Dolls agree to arbitrate or mediate their dispute. To whom might they turn for assistance? How can this assistance be located?

_____

_____

_____

15. Work through the questions for study and review at the end of the chapter in the text to reinforce your understanding.

_____

_____

_____

Chapter Review Test and Answers

Review Test

Fill in the Blank

1. The decision to accept settlement is up to _____.

2. Damages that refer to injuries preventing enjoyment of recreation, companionship, travel, etc. are called _____.

3. Pretrial conference procedure is determined by _____ _____.

4. When a case is dismissed_____ it may not be brought again.

5. Major paralegal tasks in settlement are_____, _____, and _____ material.

6. The opportunity to appeal from an arbitration decision is quite_____.

True or False

T F 1. Abilities of opposing attorneys should be researched for trial but are not important in settlement considerations.

T F 2. The settlement request usually comes from the plaintiff.

T F 3. A bid for sympathy has no place in a formal document such as the settlement request.

T F 4. In settlement, a release excuses the defendant from further liability.

T F 5. Consortium damages are calculated by this formula: value per day times days per year times years of life expectancy time percentage allowable inflation factor.

T F 6. Pain and suffering is an example of exemplary damages.

T F 7. An adjudication on the merits leaves issues that can be brought up at trial.

T F 8. Arbitration usually takes less time than a trial.

T F 9. Alternative dispute resolution is effective only in small cases.

T F 10. Early case assessment involves arbitration.

T F 11. Whether settlement agreements should be secret is controversial.

T F 12. Mandatory arbitration clauses are controversial because of a frequent disparity in bargaining power.

Multiple Choice

1. How many civil cases are settled before trial?
   a. 40–50%
   b. 20–25%
   c. 75–80%
   d. over 90–95%

2. Which is not one of the "three strikes" in evaluating an opponent's injury claim?
   a. the party has not seen a doctor
   b. the party has not been hospitalized
   c. the party has not used home remedies
   d. the party has not lost work

3. Which of the following cannot be considered in calculating damages?
   a. losses that occurred before the cause of action
   b. losses that occurred since the cause of action
   c. losses that are anticipated but have not yet occurred
   d. hedonic damages

4. Plaintiff's settlement brochure should include
   a. plaintiff's history of frequently filing injury lawsuits
   b. medical history of defendant
   c. motions and pleadings
   d. facts supported by evidence

5. In settlement the defense
   a. never proposes a settlement
   b. only reacts to the plaintiff's request
   c. seldom prepares a settlement brochure
   d. normally signs the release from liability

6. Which of the following agreement forms requires the review and approval of terms of settlement by the judge?
   a. release
   b. settlement agreement
   c. consent decree and order
   d. stipulation and order for dismissal

7. Which of the following does not relieve pressure on our court systems?
   a. arbitration
   b. adjudication on the merits
   c. mediation
   d. settlement

8. Arbitration is
   a. required by the Federal Rules of Civil Procedure
   b. not allowed in federal cases
   c. encouraged by state and federal law
   d. not allowed by most states

9. A trial de novo is a
   a. trial as if no previous hearing or arbitration had been held
   b. trial before a novice judge
   c. form of arbitration
   d. mock jury trial to assess one's case for settlement

10. Rules for mediation arise from
    a. state rules of procedure
    b. Federal Rule 38
    c. the court
    d. the participants

11. Alternative dispute resolution
    a. is seldom successful
    b. is growing as an alternative to trial
    c. does not work in family disputes
    d. is expensive

12. Ethics guidelines for mediators are contained in the
    a. ABA Model Code
    b. Federal Rule 18(b)
    c. Model Standards of Alternative Dispute Resolution
    d. Model Standards of Conduct for Mediators

Short Answer

1. What are the advantages of settlement over trial?
   _____
   _____
   _____
   _____

2. What are the ethical concerns of a paralegal discussing settlement with a client?
   _____
   _____
   _____
   _____

3. List three types of settlement requests from least to most expensive.
   _____
   _____
   _____
   _____

4. How can a video camera help in preparing for settlement?
   _____
   _____
   _____
   _____

5. Describe the usual setting and participants for a pretrial conference. List four of the summaries the paralegal should prepare for the attorney for the pretrial conference.
   _____
   _____
   _____
   _____

6. Why is it important to have the client sign an authorization for the attorney to settle?
   _____
   _____
   _____
   _____

7. What is court annexed arbitration?
   _____
   _____
   _____
   _____

8. Which of the following are true of arbitration; which true of mediation?
   a. uses statement of claim
   b. parties reach mutual agreement
   c. burden of persuasion is set
   d. is more adversarial

e. focuses on future rather than past conduct
f. can be voluntary or mandatory
g. less formal

9. Describe med–arb.

_____
_____
_____
_____

10. How does summary trial lead to settlement?

_____
_____
_____
_____

11. Define these terms: collaborative law, high-low agreement, and offer of judgment.

_____
_____
_____

Answers to Review Test

Fill in the Blank

1. the client
2. loss of enjoyment of life: LOEL
3. state or federal rules, local practice, the judge
4. with prejudice
5. gathering, organizing, and drafting
6. limited

True or False

1. F	7. F
2. T	8. T
3. F	9. F
4. T	10. F
5. T	11. T
6. F	12. T

Multiple Choice

1. d	7. b
2. b	8. c
3. a	9. a
4. d	10. d
5. c	11. b
6. c	12. d

Short Answer

1. Saves time, trouble, expense, removes uncertainty; reduces adverse publicity and animosity between parties.

2. A paralegal may not make or accept offers or counsel a client on settlement. Do not reveal harmful or confidential information.

3. Settlement letter, precis, brochure

4. "Day in the Life" videos are persuasive in establishing documentation of pain and suffering. Videos of friends and relatives regarding an injury's impact on the plaintiff and others are also helpful.

5. Judge's chambers; judge and attorneys for both sides, parties may be required to attend. (See Pretrial Conference Preparation Checklist.) Any four of the following six summaries: facts, acts, and omissions; statutes or ordinances violated; documents and other tangible evidence to be entered at trial; witnesses and testimony; all injuries, damages, and monetary amounts; and all points of factual and legal contention.

6. It allows the attorney to negotiate in good faith and is required by court decisions and rules.

7. The court controls the process, assigns a case to arbitration, and may try the case if arbitration is not successful.

8. Arbitration: a, c, d, f   Mediation: b, e, f, g

9. Alternative dispute resolution that starts as mediation and ends with arbitration of any unsettled issues.

10. It shows which side may prevail in a full-scale trial, thus encouraging the other side to settle.

11. Collaborative law: opposing attorneys work for a negotiated settlement.

   High-low agreement: maximum and minimum limits for an award are set, regardless of the jury award.

   Offer of judgment: a pretrial offer of a specific amount by defendant; if refused and the jury award is not more favorable to plaintiff, plaintiff pays defendant's costs incurred after the offer.

 For additional resources, visit our Web site at **http://www.paralegal .delmar.cengage.com.**

Chapter 11. TRIAL PREPARATION AND TRIAL

Chapter Objective

This chapter helps you become effective in working with witnesses and investigating jurors, as well as preparing and organizing the paperwork necessary to assist the attorney at trial. You will also learn the role of a paralegal at trial.

Outline

I. Trial Preparation
- A. Introduction and Trial Preparation Checklist
- B. Preliminary Trial Preparation Tasks
- C. Subpoena Witnesses
- D. Jury Investigation
  - 1. Introduction
  - 2. Sources for Juror Information
  - 3. Ancillary Investigation
- E. Preparing Demonstrative Evidence
  - 1. Introduction
  - 2. Evidentiary Concerns
  - 3. Technology
  - 4. ABA Standards
- F. Trial Notebook
  - 1. Introduction
  - 2. Legal Research
  - 3. Motions
  - 4. Voir Dire Questions
  - 5. Jury Instructions
  - 6. Witness Questions
  - 7. Juror Notebooks
  - 8. Noting Special Details
- G. Preparing the Client and Witness for Testifying at Trial
  - 1. Task
  - 2. An Ethics Reminder
- H. Additional Preparation

II. Assistance at Trial
- A. Introduction
- B. Decorum at Trial
- C. Jury Selection
- D. Shadow Jury
- E. Witness Control
- F. Documents and Exhibits
- G. Exhibit and Witness Logs
- H. Trial Notes
- I. Trial Day Review Meetings
- J. When the Paralegal Must Testify
- K. Verdict

L. Polling the Jury
M. Findings of Fact and Conclusions of Law

III. Summary

Define

In limine

_____

_____

Voir dire

_____

_____

Challenge for cause

_____

_____

Peremptory challenge

_____

_____

Prima facie case

_____

_____

Findings of fact and conclusions of law

_____

_____

Verdict

_____

_____

_____

Workbook Assignments and Exercises

System Folder Assignments

1. Expand the Trial Preparation Checklist in the text in any way recommended by your instructor and file it at the beginning of the trial preparation section of your system folder.

2. Place a list of or page reference to the steps in obtaining and serving subpoenas in your system folder. Having the list in both the deposition and trial preparations sections will prove useful.

3. Place the Juror Data Sheet or page reference to it in your system folder.

4. Reference the various sources and methods for conducting jury investigations in your system folder.

5. Locate the applicable local, state, and federal rules of evidence on demonstrative evidence. Place these in your system folder.

6.   Use the Internet or page through legal periodicals such as bar journals, *Legal Assistant Today, The National Law Journal,* and others, and develop a brief bibliography or source list of companies that prepare, sell, or rent audiovisual aids. Seek information on vendors that provide such services in your area. Add this information to your system folder.

7.   Place a copy of or page reference to the Outline of Trial Notebook in your system folder.

8.   Add copies of or references to the trial and in limine motions to both the trial and motions sections of your system folder.

9.   Draft a checklist for preparing clients and other witnesses for testifying at trial. Include a special section on preparing expert witnesses. Place the checklist in your system folder.

10. Place a copy of or page reference to the Guidelines for a Witness's Trial Testimony in your system folder.

11. Locate state examples of the three types of verdict forms and place them in an appropriate subsection of your system folder.

12. Place a copy of or page reference to the form for drafting findings of fact and conclusions of law in your system folder.

Application Assignments

1.   What special information might you want to know about jurors for the *Forrester* case? Case II?

Juror Information
Case I, Forrester Case

Pro Forrester

Pro Mercury Parcel and Hart

Case II, Ameche Case

Pro Ameche

Pro Congdens

2.   What audiovisual aids would be useful in the *Forrester* case for the plaintiff? For the defendant? Using the information that you have gathered on the scene of the accident in the *Forrester* case, prepare a courtroom diagram of the accident scene.

_____

_____

_____

_____

3.   Research form books for jury instructions in your jurisdiction. Place a list of the major sources in your system folder. Then make a list of instructions that you believe will be needed in the *Forrester* case. Compare your list to those made by others in your class.

_____

_____

_____

_____

Internet Exercises

1.   Go to the site for the ABA Civil Trial Practice Standards and download the standards to your computer screen. List the standards that address:
   a.   judicial control over trial presentations
   b.   juror note-taking
   c.   juror questioning of witnesses

2.   What does ABA Civil Trial Practice Standard 6.c recommend about availability of the verdict form?

3.   Go to the sites for the National Jury Project and the Jury Research Institute. Compare services offered and note the nature of any articles available.

Additional Learning Exercises and Discussion Points

1.   What is a case status sheet and how is it helpful in trial preparation?

_____

_____

_____

2.   How can you help prepare for objections or arguments that might arise at trial?

_____

_____

_____

3.   What are the pros and cons of subpoenaing witnesses from each side?

_____

_____

_____

4.   What is the purpose of jury investigation?

_____

_____

_____

5.   Which three of the jury investigation methods would you like to participate in and why? Show your understanding of the method and its advantages in your answer.

_____

_____

_____

6.   Draft a brief checklist of the minimum courtroom presentation equipment and backup for courtroom technology problems. Place a copy of your list in your system folder. Add a copy of or a page reference to the audio visual aids listed in the technology subsection of the chapter. If not provided otherwise, seek an opportunity to use some presentation technology. Some campus technology labs have this equipment and software.

_____

_____

_____

7.   Describe research and writing tasks that a paralegal can do in preparing the trial notebook.

_____

_____

_____

8.   In a role-playing situation, familiarize a classmate/witness with a mock courtroom and offer guidance for trial testimony. Discuss clothing, demeanor, and techniques and ethics for answering questions.

_____

_____

_____

9.   What miscellaneous tasks can a paralegal do to help things go smoothly for the legal team outside the courtroom during trial?

_____

_____

_____

10. Briefly, what are the stages in trial procedure? (Exhibit 11:11)

_____

_____

_____

11. Compare and contrast a trial and an arbitration hearing.

_____

_____

_____

12. Prepare a list of paralegal tasks to assist the attorney at trial.

_____

_____

_____

13. Briefly describe the elements of good paralegal decorum at trial stated in the text. Add any suggestions from your instructor.

_____

_____

_____

14. Work through the questions for study and review at the end of the chapter in the text to reinforce your understanding.

_____

_____

_____

Chapter Review Test and Answers

Review Test

Fill in the Blank

1. Reviewing the case with the attorney as the trial nears can help you _____ _____ _____.

2. In the federal system a motion for a directed verdict is called _____ _____.

3. Jury investigation is a preparation for _____.

4. Mock juries can help the attorney decide _____ and _____.

5. A courtroom bar code reader can be used to _____.

True or False

T F 1. The case status sheet should be started in the month before trial.

T F 2. The judge usually determines whether the jury is allowed to take notes, have mid-trial discussions, or ask questions of witnesses.

T F 3. Professional jury services are expensive and not very helpful in jury investigation.

T F 4. A good rule of thumb is to use demonstrative evidence whether you think it will help or not.

T F 5. The best practice is to subpoena all witnesses necessary to prove your case.

T F 6. Peremptory challenges are unlimited in number.

T F 7. Instant transcript reporting allows the legal team to make changes to the transcript from laptop computers.

T F 8. Subpoenas may be obtained at the last minute before trial.

T F 9. It is unethical to research the background of the trial judge.

T F 10. A trial notebook should contain all the evidence gathered through discovery.

Multiple Choice

1. A case status sheet shows the
   a. legal team how their case will look to a jury
   b. judge how soon the case will be ready for trial
   c. legal team what is left to be done
   d. opposition how strong your case is

2. Subpoenas need to be reissued if
   a. there is a change of venue
   b. there is a postponement
   c. they are challenged
   d. the trial lasts longer than a week

3. Which of the following is not a function or use of a juror data sheet?
   a. a summary sheet for the attorney during voir dire
   b. a paralegal's checklist to determine what information to gather
   c. a record of juror experiences related to trial issues
   d. a checklist for jurors to keep track of evidence during trial

4. Which of the following is the best method of jury investigation if costs must be kept to a minimum?
   a. jury surveys
   b. jury information sheets
   c. mock jury
   d. juror interviews

5. Demonstrative evidence
   a. may sometimes help the other side more than your own
   b. is too expensive for most cases
   c. is less important to today's jurors
   d. always requires professional preparation

6. To be admissible, demonstrative evidence must
   a. be an exact representation
   b. be stipulated by your opponent
   c. have evidentiary foundation
   d. be under subpoena duces tecum

7. Differences in preparing a client for trial as opposed to depositions include
   a. more communication with client
   b. familiarizing client with courtroom
   c. advising client on clothing choice
   d. all of the above

8. If you know that a witness plans to lie under oath
   a. it is the witness's concern
   b. it is the attorney's concern
   c. it is your concern
   d. all of the above

9. A paralegal may be responsible for
   a. pointing out areas of witness examination missed by the attorney
   b. deciding when to enter a motion in limine
   c. questioning jurors at voir dire
   d. extensive out-of-court interaction with jurors

10. Translating body language
    a. is the most helpful tool in jury selection
    b. should be done with caution
    c. is based on irrefutable scientific study
    d. all of the above

11. Shadow juries
    a. are required by Federal Rule 47
    b. can be helpful in preparing the closing argument
    c. can not be managed by paralegals
    d. are allowed only by leave of the court

12. In preparing witnesses for trial, it is important to
    a. be tactful
    b. tell them all the details of the case
    c. keep them from knowing how other witnesses are likely to testify
    d. tell them to look at the attorney when answering questions

13. A well-prepared paralegal will take into the courtroom
    a. hard copy backups of all exhibits
    b. a cell phone for frequent office communication
    c. no duplicate materials, to reduce confusion
    d. a new designer handbag, to impress the jury

14. A special verdict is one that
    a. sets punitive damages
    b. the judge decides based on findings of fact by the jury
    c. the jury decides based on directions from the judge
    d. finds for the plaintiff, but awards no damages

15. A general verdict
    a. must be consistent with answers to interrogatories from the judge
    b. is decided by the judge
    c. results in a new trial
    d. indicates the amount of any award if the plaintiff wins

Short Answer

1. If the judge for your trial follows a docket list, what must you watch for?
   _____
   _____
   _____

2. What do you need to remember about identifying documents on a subpoena duces tecum?
   _____
   _____
   _____

3. What can you learn about potential jurors from voter registration lists? Jury surveys?
   _____
   _____
   _____

4. Besides the jury, who else should be researched before the trial?
   _____
   _____
   _____

5. What factors can help make diagrams effective for use at trial? What has simplified the preparation and enhanced the quality of timeline diagrams?

_____

_____

_____

6. How can a late start be a help in preparing a trial notebook?

_____

_____

_____

7. How is a motion in limine used?

_____

_____

_____

8. How can you prepare an expert witness for testimony at trial?

_____

_____

_____

9. What are the grounds for a judgment notwithstanding the verdict (a renewal of the motion for judgment as a matter of law)?

_____

_____

_____

10. What are the elements of good paralegal decorum at trial?

_____

_____

_____

Answers to Review Test

Fill in the Blank

1. verify issues, review evidence, and pinpoint needs for further research
2. a motion for judgment as a matter of law
3. voir dire
4. what jurors to select, how to improve their presentation
5. identify and project an exhibit

True or False

1. F   6. F
2. T   7. F
3. F   8. T
4. F   9. F
5. T   10. F

Multiple Choice

1. c   6. c   11. b
2. a   7. d   12. a
3. d   8. d   13. a
4. b   9. a   14. b
5. a   10. b   15. d

Short Answer

1. How your case is moving up on the docket as other cases are tried or settled so you will know when the trial is likely to start; so everyone can be informed and prepared.

2. They must be described with reasonable certainty, making extensive searches unnecessary. Words such as "every" or "all" are suspect.

3. Political party affiliations, where required. Attitudes of a community toward the issues at trial, especially the attitudes of those individuals who match prospective jurors' backgrounds.

4. Judge, opposing counsel, community

5. Simplicity, accuracy, readability. Specific timeline creation software.

6. Issues are already narrowed by discovery and pretrial conference, so there will be fewer witnesses and less evidence to present.

7. To ask the court's protection against questions the opponent is likely to ask that will prejudice the jury.

8. Collect and summarize qualifications, provide facts and theories of the case, note expert's suggestions for material needed, guide against defensiveness, jargon, condescension.

9. The verdict is against the great weight of the evidence, or, as a matter of law, there is only one reasonable conclusion for the verdict.

10. Prior to trial, discuss decorum with your supervising attorney; dress as a professional representative, conservatively but comfortably; reflect confidence in client, witnesses, and colleagues; respect court guidelines for e-communication devices, use during recesses; and avoid personal interaction with jurors.

 For additional resources, visit our Web site at **http://www.paralegal .delmar.cengage.com.**

Chapter 12. POST-TRIAL PRACTICE FROM MOTIONS TO APPEAL

Chapter Objective

This chapter provides the necessary background and skills for you to effectively assist in preparing post-trial motions, enforcing judgments, and appealing cases.

Outline

Define

Judgment creditor

_____

_____

Judgment debtor

_____

_____

Lis pendens

_____

_____

Judgment proof

_____

_____

Post-judgment interrogatory

_____

_____

Post-trial request for production of documents

_____

_____

Post-trial deposition

_____

_____

Supplementary proceedings

_____

_____

Supersedeas bond

_____

_____

Execution

_____

_____

Levy

_____

_____

Receivership

_____

_____

Garnishment

_____

_____

Garnishee

_____

_____

Exemplified

_____

_____

Question of law

_____

_____

Question of fact

_____

_____

Harmless error

_____

_____

Workbook Assignments and Exercises

System Folder Assignments

1.   Enter the 10-day time limit for filing post-trial motions in the Motions, Pleadings, and Time Limits exhibit in Chapter 6. Place copies of or page references to the motions in your system folder, both in a post-trial motion section and in your motion practice section. Indicate what federal and state rules govern the motions.

2.   Place a page reference to or a copy of the Bill of Costs in your system folder. If your state has a similar form, include it. Note the applicable state and federal rules.

3.   Research the rules of procedure and law in your jurisdiction on the availability of formal supplementary proceedings for locating a judgment debtor's assets. Check the U.S. Code as well for any such procedures. Then list the procedures and applicable rules and statutes in your system folder. Place a copy of or a page reference to the notice of lis pendens and the interrogatories in Aid of Judgment in your system folder.

4.   Research your state law to determine what assets of a judgment debtor are exempt from execution on the judgment. List these in your system folder.

5.   Research the forms and procedures for garnishment in your state. Make a checklist and place it and copies of or references to the appropriate forms in your system folder.

6.   Make an outline of the procedure for domesticating a judgment in another state and in federal court. Place the outline in your system folder.

7.   Check the law library for form and procedure books on enforcement of judgments or collections for your state. Draft a step-by-step checklist for enforcing a judgment in your state. Place the checklist and any pertinent forms in your system folder.

8.   Place a page reference or copy of the Checklist for Federal Appellate Procedure (Appellant) in your system folder. Research appellate procedure for your state and make a separate state appellate checklist for your system folder. Verify appellate time requirements in the Motions, Pleadings, and Time Limits exhibit and add state time limits.

9.   Place page references or a copy of the skeletal appellate brief in your system folder. Enter applicable rule references. Research the format of an appellate brief for your state. Include a copy in your system folder plus references to rules on the required format.

10. Complete your litigation system folder, update its table of contents, and prepare it for grading.

Application Assignments

1.   Assume that your client has a judgment for $250,000 against X, who lives in your state. You know that X has $100,000 in liability insurance, a $100,000 home and land, a small cottage worth $60,000 (but only $15,000 paid for), two vehicles each worth $10,000 (both paid for), a boat worth $7,000, and an online coffee business that generates $30,000 in gross annual income. Under your state statutes, what of X's assets are not exempt from execution on the judgment?

_____

_____

_____

_____

2.   Assume that you represent a judgment debtor who has recently paid off a judgment. Under your state law, what procedure must one follow to record a release of judgment?

_____

_____

_____

_____

3.   When must a notice of appeal be filed under your state's rule of appellate procedure? Can this time be extended by the court?

_____

_____

_____

_____

Internet Exercises

1.   Go to http://www.ca6.uscourts.gov. What types of information does this site have or link to that would help you if you had an appellate case in the 6th Circuit?

2.   Substituting your circuit number for the 6 in the Web site in Internet Exercise 1, what helpful information is available for appellate practice in your circuit?

3.   Go to the North Dakota court site, enter "briefs" in the search space, go to the _Lang v. Binstock_ case and click on related documents, then click on the appellant brief for that case. Outline the sections of the brief and restate the two issues in question.

Additional Learning Exercises and Discussion Points

1.   What is the consequence for failing to renew a motion for judgment as a matter of law and a motion for new trial under the _Unitherm Food_ case?

_____

_____

_____

2.   If a defendant has moved for a judgment as a matter of law (directed verdict) based on the weight of the evidence and the motion was denied, what motion may the defendant file after the trial if the defendant believes the jury's verdict is against the weight of the evidence? What motion should be filed if the defendant believes a serious procedural error was committed by the judge? What state rules govern these motions?

_____

_____

_____

3.   Assume for purposes of this assignment that, contrary to the weight of the evidence, the jury returned a verdict against Ms. Forrester. The areas that you believe the jury ignored are a) that Hart was looking at the van radio just prior to the accident; b) that several of Mercury Parcel's documents showed the van had faulty brakes; and c) that defendants offered no evidence whatsoever that Ms. Forrester was careless or contributed in any way to the accident. Using your state form, draft a motion (no supporting affidavit or memorandum) for judgment notwithstanding the verdict.

_____
_____
_____

4.   Work through the questions for study and review at the end of the chapter in the text to reinforce your understanding.

_____
_____
_____

Chapter Review Test and Answers

Review Test

Fill in the Blank

1. Common devices to set aside judgment are (state)_____ and (federal)
    _____.

2. The bill of costs is filed by _____.

3. Three discovery devices that can be helpful in post-judgment investigations include
    _____
    _____.

4. The least expensive collection method is_____.

5. The Federal Fair Trade Debt Collections Practices Act is important to a paralegal writ-
    ing a letter to _____.

6. The trial transcript is sent to the appellate court by_____.

True or False

T F 1.   Motions to have a judgment set aside must be filed right after the verdict is read.

T F 2.   Motions for judgment as a matter of law and for a new trial must be renewed to
          preserve the issue for appeal.

T F 3.   It is best to wait to compile bills and costs until a case is decided, so that everything
          can be included at one time.

T F 4.   Prejudgment remedies are less popular than they used to be.

T F 5.   Payment of the judgment amount is due within 10 days of the verdict.

T F 6.   Most appeals are unsuccessful.

T F 7.   An experienced paralegal can assume the role of appeals manager.

T F 8.   The jury decides questions of law.

T F 9.   Receivership secures the amount of judgment pending post-trial motions.

T F 10. Up to 25 percent of disposable earnings can be garnished.

T F 11. Appeal procedure is found in Federal Rule for Civil Procedure 54.

T F 12. In the federal system, the notice of appeal is filed in the appellate court.

T F 13. Unpublished opinions issued after January 1, 2007, may be cited in federal appeals.

Multiple Choice

1. Who may file a motion for JNOV under Rule 50?
    a. the loser of the case
    b. the defendant when there were procedural errors
    c. the party who has a cause of action
    d. the party who has moved for a directed verdict

2. The bill of costs includes
   a. attorneys' fees
   b. witness fees
   c. special damages
   d. costs of jury investigation

3. Which of these is intangible property?
   a. royalties rights of an author
   b. lien
   c. a diamond ring
   d. a certificate of deposit

4. Creditor's examinations have the advantage of
   a. flexibility
   b. being inexpensive
   c. reaching a variety of documents
   d. being quick

5. An example of a self-executing judgment is
   a. transfer of a deed
   b. payment of $10,000
   c. divorce
   d. return of a painting

6. Debtor's property held by a third party can be obtained through
   a. receivership
   b. garnishment
   c. domestication
   d. bill of costs

7. Lis pendens is
   a. a record that plaintiff has asserted a claim against property
   b. the process of securing property for the judgment creditor
   c. a motion included with the appellate brief
   d. a post-trial deposition

8. A prejudgment remedy
   a. is an early verdict
   b. is a directed verdict
   c. prevents the defendant from selling assets
   d. prevents the need to go to trial

9. A lien is
   a. the term for domesticating a judgment
   b. intangible property
   c. recoverable in the bill of costs
   d. the same as a mortgage in some states

10. An example of a question of fact is
    a. was the letter admissible evidence
    b. was the road icy the day of the accident
    c. were jury instructions proper
    d. was the statute constitutional

11. Appeals are based on
    a. questions of fact
    b. questions of law
    c. questions of intent
    d. all of the above

12. If harmless error occurred at trial
    a. the appeal will be successful
    b. a new trial will be granted
    c. the verdict will stand
    d. the matter will be mediated

13. Which of the following does not provide guidance in writing appellate briefs?
    a. Federal Rules of Appellate Procedure 28, 30, and 32
    b. appellate handbooks
    c. briefs for other cases
    d. guide to post-judgment enforcement

14. Parties are expected to agree on
    a. contents of the appendix to the appellate brief
    b. issues under appeal
    c. questions of law
    d. questions of fact

15. The form for the appellate brief and appendices is
    a. up to the appellant
    b. regulated in detail by Federal Rule
    c. determined by the appellate judge
    d. determined by the trial judge

Short Answer

1. What are three grounds for a motion for a new trial?

   _____

   _____

   _____

2. When are plaintiffs allowed to seize defendants' property before a trial?

   _____

   _____

   _____

3. Why is it important to determine a defendant's assets early in a case?

   _____

   _____

   _____

4. Under what circumstances will an appellate judge review evidence?

   _____

   _____

   _____

5. In what areas is a paralegal's assistance especially effective in appeals practice?

   _____

   _____

   _____

Answers to Review Test

Fill in the Blank

1. motion for judgment notwithstanding the verdict, renewal of motion for judgment as a matter of law, motion for a new trial
2. the prevailing party
3. interrogatories, production of documents, and depositions (creditor's examination)
4. a letter
5. collect payment of a judgment for a personal debt
6. the appellant

True or False		*Multiple Choice*		
1. F	8. F	1. d	6. b	11. b
2. T	9. F	2. b	7. a	12. c
3. F	10. T	3. a	8. c	13. d
4. T	11. F	4. a	9. d	14. a
5. F	12. F	5. c	10. b	15. b
6. T	13. T			
7. T				

Short Answer

1. Procedural errors, verdict contrary to law, excessive or inadequate damages.

2. When it is likely that defendant will try to hide or transfer assets to avoid loss.

3. If there are no or few assets, the case may not be worth the trouble.

4. When appeal is on the issue of whether the verdict goes against the weight of the evidence.

5. Management, research, verifying the record, appellate brief, oral argument.

   For additional resources, visit our Web site at **http://www.paralegal .delmar.cengage.com.**

Notes:

Notes:

Notes:

Notes:

Notes:

Notes:

Notes:

Notes:

Notes: